WALLACE STEVENS

FR

OLIVER AND BOYD

EDINBURGH AND LONDON

OLIVER AND BOYD LTD
Tweeddale Court
Edinburgh 1

39A Welbeck Street
London W.1

First published 1960
Reprinted 1967

Printed in Great Britain for Oliver and Boyd Ltd
by Robert MacLehose and Co. Ltd, Glasgow.

CONTENTS

ACKNOWLEDGMENTS

Acknowledgment is due to Faber and Faber Ltd and to Alfred A. Knopf, Inc., for permission to reproduce all quotations from the works of Wallace Stevens, including: *The Collected Poems of Wallace Stevens* (copyright 1954 Wallace Stevens); *The Necessary Angel* (copyright 1951 Wallace Stevens); *Opus Posthumous* (copyright 1957 Elsie Stevens and Holly Stevens).

Acknowledgments are also due to the following publishers for permission to quote from the works indicated: A. and C. Black Ltd (George Santayana, *The Sense of Beauty*); Chatto and Windus Ltd (Marius Bewley, *The Complex Fate*); Columbia University Press (*Literature and Belief*, English Institute Essays 1957, article by Louis Martz in *Yale Review*); Constable and Co., Ltd, and Charles Scribner's Sons (George Santayana, *Interpretations of Poetry and Religion* and *The Sense of Beauty*); Faber and Faber Ltd (Randall Jarrell, *Poetry of the Age*); The Modern Language Association of America (article by Roy Harvey Pearce); Henry Regnery Company (W. Van O'Connor, *The Shaping Spirit*); Routledge and Kegan Paul Ltd (Paul Valéry, *Collected Works*); Allan Swallow (Yvor Winters, *In Defense of Reason*).

Several passages of this book have appeared in a somewhat different form in *Encounter* and the *Spectator*, and thanks are due to the Editors of those Journals for permission to use this material.

Acknowledgments are also due to Alfred A. Knopf, Inc., and John Haley for supplying a print of the photograph of Wallace Stevens reproduced on the front cover.

F. K.

LIST OF ABBREVIATED TITLES
BY WHICH WALLACE STEVENS' WORKS
ARE CITED IN REFERENCES

C.P.	=	*The Collected Poems of Wallace Stevens*, New York 1954, London 1955.
N.S.F.	=	*Notes Toward a Supreme Fiction*, *C.P.*, pp. 380–408.
O.E.N.H.	=	*An Ordinary Evening in New Haven*, *C.P.*, pp. 465–489.
N.A.	=	*The Necessary Angel*, New York 1951, London 1960.
"N.R."	=	"The Noble Rider and the Sound of Words," *N.A.*, pp. 3–36.
"F.Y.V.P."	=	"The Figure of the Youth as Virile Poet," *N.A.*, pp. 39–67.
"I.V."	=	"Imagination as Value," *N.A.*, pp. 133–56.
"R.P.P."	=	"The Relation between Poetry and Painting," *N.A.*, pp. 159–76.
O.P.	=	*Opus Posthumous*, New York 1957, London 1959.

CHAPTER I

LIFE

Wallace Stevens, as even hostile critics admit, is a deeply interesting poet; in time, therefore, his life will be written down. Samuel French Morse is at work on a critical biography authorised by the poet's widow and his daughter, and has given some hints of the quality of this book in the Preface to *Opus Posthumous* (1957, 1959)—a collection of the poet's work omitted from, or written too late for, the *Collected Poems* (1954, 1955) and *The Necessary Angel* (1951, 1960).[1] Morse's book will do much to augment the scattered and casual biographical information that is at present available; but in the nature of the case—as we shall see—it is unlikely to throw much light on an aspect of Stevens which has attracted much attention: the divorce between his activities as a man of business, a family man, a citizen of Hartford, Connecticut, and his work as a man of letters. This issue gets, I think, too much attention of the wrong kind, and even critics one would normally consider free of obvious vulgarity have allowed their judgment of the poetry to be corrupted by wonder or annoyance at the poet's double life. Stevens did not find that he must choose between the careers of insurance lawyer and poet. The fork in the road where he took the wrong turning is a critic's invention, and there is no point in dawdling there. Still, Stevens' life has for long stretches run remote from men who keep diaries and gossip about poets and poetry. In what follows I simply repeat some of the known facts and add some comments of a kind that might be useful in a preliminary chapter.[2]

Stevens was born in Reading, Pennsylvania, on 2 Oct.

1879, the son of a lawyer. His mother's maiden name was Zeller; according to Stevens his ancestry on that side was Dutch. In a rare autobiographical excursion Stevens, in 1948, wrote:

Life, not the artist, creates or reveals reality: time and experience in the poet, in the painter. During last September, I visited the old Zeller house in the Tulpehocken, in Pennsylvania. This family of religious refugees came to this country in 1709, lived for some fifteen or twenty years in the Scoharie region in New York and then went down the Susquehanna to the valley in which the house was built. Over the door there is an architectural cartouche of the cross with palm-branches below, placed there, no doubt, to indicate that the house and those that lived in it were consecrated to the glory of God. From this doorway they faced the hills that were part of the frame of their valley, the familiar shelter in which they spent their laborious lives, happy in the faith and worship in which they rejoiced. Their reality consisted of both the visible and the invisible. . . . [He goes with an old Lutheran into the graveyard of Trinity Tulpehocken Reformed Church.] This was an enclosure of about an acre, possibly a little more. The wall was of limestone about four feet high, weather-beaten, barren, bald. In the graveyard were possibly eight or ten sheep, the colour of the wall and of many of the gravestones and even of some of the tufts of grass, bleached and silvery in the hard sunlight. The droppings of the sheep fertilized the soil. There were a few cedars here and there but these only accentuated the sense of abandonment and destitution, the sense that, after all, the vast mausoleum of human memory is emptier than one had supposed. . . . Although the two elderly men were in a way a diversion from the solitude, there could not be any effective diversion from the reality that time and experience had

created here, the desolation that penetrated one like
something final.[3]

This seems to me an instructive parable. It is a fundamental principle for Stevens that there exists no difference
between poetry and the *materia poetica*; a poem is reality
discovered or revealed in the experience of the artist.
"Poetry means not the language of poetry but the thing
itself, wherever it may be found."[4] Consequently the
poetry of Stevens is a finding of reality in his own experience; his life is a discovering of poetry. "The collect-
ing of poetry from one's experience as one goes along is
not the same thing as merely writing poetry."[5] It is, however, not his custom often to allude to specific experiences,
even in his prose (which is structurally close kin to his
verse); and when he does so, as in this passage, he is
invariably meditating—using the experience as a starting
point for what may become a poem (a discovery of
reality) or a critical essay (a discovery of poetry). In
the present instance the experience resulted in both: this
passage from an essay on Marianne Moore; and two
poems, "Dutch Graves in Bucks County" and "The Bed
of Old John Zeller," which were published in *Transport
to Summer* (1947). We shall encounter further examples of
the same process.

The nature of this prose meditation is complex; for it
arises from a consideration of Marianne Moore's poem
about the ostrich ("He 'Digesteth Hard Yron' ") in relation to some observations of Mr H. D. Lewis "On Poetic
Truth." Miss Moore, digesting the hard iron of finical
fact, seems to demonstrate Mr Lewis's point, that to extract a meaning from a poem is a mistake "due to en-
thusiasm for moral or religious truth." What is said in
the poem is important, "but . . . only in so far as the
saying of that particular something in a special way is a
revelation of reality." Stevens accepts the conclusion of
Mr Lewis concerning the affinity between art and reli-

gion today: "both have to mediate for us a reality not ourselves. . . . This is what the poet does. . . . The supreme virtue here is humility, for the humble are they that move about the world with the lure of the real in their hearts."[6] Then he tells the story of the Zeller house, because it makes this, and some related points. The Zellers had a religion which penetrated their lives and the place where they lived, so that the visible and the invisible were held together in the same thought. The graveyard where they lie becomes an emblem of the emptiness which is all that is left for the poet of that achievement in living, creating, worshipping, and rejoicing; the reality of the place is now desolation, because of change and decay. What takes the place of the old myth by which the Zellers recognised reality? Poetry— "within it there may yet be found a reality adequate to the profound necessities of life today or for that matter any day."[7] Miss Moore's delicate imagination transports her, as she observes the ostrich, "into the presence of a recognizable reality, because, as it happens, she has the faculty of digesting the 'harde yron' of appearance."[8]

The house and the graveyard, Miss Moore and Mr Lewis, are caught up into a meditation on the supreme, the sustaining fiction, on poetry as "the one reality | In this imagined world"[9]—on Stevens' central theme. In "Dutch Graves" he addresses his dead kin in a time of war and chaos: they are "doubly killed | To be buried in desert and deserted earth." They are dead, "mossy cronies," "haggard with past thought"; their "ecstasy | Was the glory of heaven in the wilderness," but "the stars . . . | Shine on the very living of those alive." Nevertheless,

Time was not wasted in your subtle temples.
No: nor divergence made too steep to follow down.

And he addressed the dead throughout as "my semblables."[10] By their vision they made an order out of chaos; among the "violent marchers of the present" he would wish to do the same. Change is the law of Stevens' world; the graveyard suggests that

> the mobs of birth
> Avoid our stale perfections, seeking out
> Their own, waiting until we go
> To picnic in the ruins that we leave.

"The Bed of Old John Zeller" is a more tightly made poem on the topic of the difference between Zeller's reality and the one the modern poet must recognise. One may wish, "as if one's grandfather lay | In one's heart and wished as he had always wished," for obsolete, beautifully structured accounts of reality. But

> It is more difficult to evade
> That habit of wishing and to accept the structure
> Of things as the structure of ideas.

This is the theme of the first poem in the third section of Stevens' greatest work, *Notes toward a Supreme Fiction*: it is one thing "To sing jubilas at exact, accustomed times" and another to imagine and so transform reality. Poets need the vision of the Zellers; the material of poetry must be reality, not myth; yet poetry must "take the place | Of empty heaven and its hymns."[11]

We grow accustomed to the multiple interlacing of Stevens' poems—to their repetitiousness, indeed, for he was not afraid of being thought repetitive. There is behind the poems one life, and some few ways of thinking about that life. A visit to the Zeller house provokes no childhood memories, no pride of kin; nothing of "human interest" at all, except in a higher sense than the words usually have. The lure of reality might take you to places there is no need to specify exactly—

> among the cigar stores,
> Ryan's lunch, hatters, insurance and medicines—[12]

but here the specific did matter, for Zeller was a religious man and lay in that graveyard, and might, if such a thing is possible, have something in common with his descendant. Yet "the reek of the human" is absent from Stevens; this lack becomes a critical issue to which I shall return. For the present, it is enough to add that being this kind of man Stevens did not broadcast the details of his private life.

Stevens was at Harvard from 1897 to 1900. He planned to go to Paris and write; but after a short time as a reporter on the *New York Herald Tribune* he went to the New York Law School, where he graduated in 1903. In the following year he was admitted to the New York Bar and practised in New York City until 1916. He set himself with determination to the task of being a successful lawyer, though he wrote some poems as an undergraduate, as well as some prose for the *Harvard Advocate*,[13] and later had friends among the writers and painters of Greenwich Village. He knew, among others, William Carlos Williams, Marianne Moore and E. E. Cummings, and he took part in their projects and entertainments, though "always in a distant manner, shyly, unwilling to be active or vocal. . . . He was always the well-dressed one, diffident about letting down his hair. Precise when we were sloppy. Drank little. . . . But we all knew, liked and admired him. He really was felt to be part of the gang."[14]

Of his early verses Stevens said that they gave him the creeps.[15] We do not know whether he continued to write poetry; "of the poems surviving in manuscript, the earliest belongs to 1913."[16] A number of lyrics written soon after this he grouped together under the title "Phases."[17] They refer obliquely to the 1914 war and could not be called distinguished. Under the pseudonym of "Peter Parasol," Stevens sent "Phases" to Harriet Monroe, editor of *Poetry*, as an entry for a war-poem competition. He did not win the prize; but Miss Monroe liked the poems and printed four of the eleven. She remembered that she had to reassemble the page-proofs of the War Number of *Poetry* in order to squeeze in even four pieces by "this master of strange and beautiful rhythms," they arrived so late; and she claims for *Poetry* the honour of introducing Stevens to the public.[18] Later, although he contributed to Kreymborg's rival periodical *Others* (1915–1916: poems included "Peter Quince at the Clavier"), Stevens continued the association with Harriet Monroe. He allowed her to reprint "Fallen Winkle" in her anthology *The New Poetry*; more important, he published the first version of "Sunday Morning," his most celebrated poem, in her journal (Nov. 1915).

At the time of "Phases" Stevens was thirty-five, "a big, slightly fat, awfully competent man. You expect him to roar, but when he speaks there emerges the gravest, softest, most subtly modulated voice I've ever heard," in the words of Arthur Ficke. Miss Monroe spoke of his "quiet power" and "the flicker of humour playing on deep pools of understanding," finding Stevens "super-sensitive to beauty but incased in the protective armour of the business attorney."[19] She indulged Stevens' dramatic ambitions and published his two short plays *Carlos among the Candles* (1917) and *Three Travellers Watch the Sunrise* (1916), which won a prize in a verse-play competition. The plays are interesting, though much of their period: "a theatre without action or characters"[20] derives from Symbolist theory and perhaps especially from Mallarmé, though the Japanese Nō was also enjoying a great vogue at the time. The imagery of the candles in *Carlos* recurs near the end of Stevens' life in the beautiful "Final Soliloquy of the Interior Paramour" (*C.P.*, p. 524). And the language of *Three Travellers* also looks forward to mature Stevens:

> All you need,
> To find poetry,
> Is to look for it with a lantern.[21]

But when all is said, the plays are not obviously the work of an exceptional poet; and "Sunday Morning," which is, had not yet reached its final form. Stevens was by any normal standard a rather slow starter.

But now he was becoming more prolific. In 1916 he moved to Hartford, Connecticut, and joined the Hartford Accident and Indemnity Company, of which he became Vice-President in 1934; he remained in Hartford, and with the Company, until his death on 2 Aug. 1955. Ostensibly his main object was success in this career; but he kept up with his New York friends, and between mid-1916 and the end of 1917 published about a poem a month. Some of these appear in the first collection; others have been rescued in *Opus Posthumous*. The fifteen poems of 1918 include the series *Lettres d'un Soldat*, rejected from the *Collected Poems*[22] but very characteristic of the poet's Francophile mood; and also the major poem "Le Monocle de mon Oncle." In 1919, after a vacation in Florida, he seems to have produced a good deal, including the Florida poems in *Harmonium*. And so he went on; between 1914 and 1923 he published "about 100 poems," according to the count of O'Connor;[23] and about 74 survive in the *Collected Poems*, including the long poem "The Comedian as the Letter C."

Stevens had fully matured what we shall have to call his early manner or manners—the "gaudy" language with many gallicisms and out-of-the-way words, the freak titles, the colour symbols, the style devised for Imagist scraps and the longer meditative style. And already his poetry was clearly, under one form or another, *about* poetry and, though remarkably unpredictable—for if poetry is what one finds, it depends heavily on the fortuitous—it bore the mark of what Stevens later called "the thing that is incessantly overlooked: ... the presence of the determining personality." "Without that reality," he added, "no amount of other things matters much."[24] He was by now well known, and had written some—perhaps most—of the poetry on which his later and higher reputation was to depend. But he remained elusive if not aloof. "Who is Mr. Stevens?" asked Amy Lowell. "Tell me something about him."[25] According to Kreymborg, his friends were urging him to publish a book; W. C. Williams records Stevens' celebrated observation, "Well, a book of poems is a damned serious affair."[26] By 1922 he had contracted to prepare a book— "a collection of things that have already appeared," he called it[27]—and he revised the long grotesque-doctrinal poem "The Comedian as the Letter C." The business of making a book produced some characteristic comment from the poet:

> I know that people judge one by volume. However, having elected to regard poetry as a form of retreat, the judgment of people is neither here nor there. The desire to write a long poem or two is not obsequiousness to the judgment of people. On the contrary, I find that this prolonged attention to a single subject has the same result that prolonged attention to a senora has, according to the authorities. All manner of favors drop from it. Only it requires a skill in the varying of the serenade.[28]

Stevens, we note, still thought of himself as a scanty poet (a view still held—oddly, in view of the bulk of the *Collected Poems*) and was turning his thoughts, as he revised "The Comedian," to long poems; the Romantic meditation was in its way as suitable to his mood as the brief Imagist lyric. As he put the book together and felt depressed at its quality, he repeated that long poems offered the chance he needed. "The reading of these outmoded and debilitated poems does make me wish rather desperately to keep on dabbling and to be as obscure as possible until I have perfected an authentic and fluent speech for myself."[29]

On this issue of the long poem Stevens was, I think,

shrewd. He did need it. In the end, after some failures,
it yielded him more favours than any other poet of the
century. As for the poems that so depressed him, he
edited them with great care; and in 1923 Knopf published *Harmonium*. It had on the whole a poor critical
reception, and not many copies were sold—though it
was praised by some reviewers, including Marianne
Moore and Mark van Doren.

Harmonium will be considered below; but at this point
it may be proper to answer the question as to what this
poet of forty-four had been reading and looking at, or
what had he nourished his talent, during these years of
writing. When a talent grows in relative isolation, and
when the personality is fastidious and modest, one may
expect no crude reflexion of the fashionable styles and
masters, no influence that is not subjected to what
Stevens in 1917 called the desirable achievement: "a
single manner or mood thoroughly matured."[30] Everything else, he argued, will adjust itself to this "fixed point
of view." And although it is clear that Stevens was
affected by the Imagists, by French poetry, by Whitman
—and that later he felt the influence of Eliot and many
others—the strong tang of a highly individual consciousness penetrates even the earlier work, to the degree that
we can tell a Stevens failure as we detect the rottenness of
a particular fruit: it is bad in its own peculiar way, a
corruption of the good, an evil parody of banana.

That he was much affected by French poetry is certain
and not at all unexpected. In May 1920 John Gould
Fletcher, introducing Stevens to English readers, said of
Stevens that his work "recalls Mallarmé or Villiers
de l'Isle Adam, and in some ageless drama like *Axël* or
Hérodiade he might be most at home."[31] This is over-
stated; but the comparison with Mallarmé's poem at
least is accurate, at any rate for the earlier period, when
a controlled "decadence" of language is part of Stevens'
method. Indeed it remained so. There is no reason to

'ispute the general opinion that Mallarmé, Verlaine,
nd Laforgue were assimilated by Stevens and power-
ily affected *Harmonium*.[32] The influence of Valéry, who
is almost Stevens' contemporary, became more power-
i later. There is nothing out of the way in this preoccu-
ation with French poetry; indeed it was practically
escapable. The *avant-garde* interests of the period, in
merica as well as in England, were to a great extent
sorbed by French culture: painting, dancing, music
d poetry. A Symbolist aesthetic, in itself a specialisa-
on of its Romantic forebear, dominated all the arts; the
nagism of Pound and Williams was, despite disclaimers,
nly a local version of it. Questioned by the French
cholar René Taupin, Stevens wrote that "the lightness,
he grace, the sound and the colour of French have had
n undeniable and precious influence upon me." Taupin
ightly infers that this linguistic influence could hardly
xist without some accompanying literary effect. "It is
not only that Stevens employs French vocabulary," says
Taupin, "the movement of his sentences is French. It
makes more use of exclamations and questions than is
usual in English poetry." And he goes on to argue that
Stevens writes in the French tradition: "his desire for
elegance, his dandyism, relates him to Baudelaire, his
nonchalant irony—*le ton 'pierrot'*—to Laforgue, even if
his Pierrot is dressed in black and carries a silk hat."
Finally, says Taupin, "he is Symbolist by reason of his
evocatory art, his search for *correspondances*, for words
which constitute images and words which reverberate
with associations." Taupin also tells us that Stevens translated some French poems, he does not say which. There
is no saying what they were; the only available examples
of Stevens as a translator are the very late (1951) "para-
phrases" of Léon-Paul Fargue and an isolated version of
a poem by Jean Le Roy called "Moment of Light,"
which he published in 1918.[33]

The French interests of Stevens were, then, strong from

the start to the finish of his career. "French and English
constitute a single language," he wrote in the *Adagia*[34]—
a view which has earned him some obloquy, and which is
in any case more obviously applicable to his own dialect
than to the dialect of the tribe. Large borrowings from
French are part of the general fantastication of English
which goes on in Stevens; they take their place beside all
the archaisms and neologisms that critics like to make
lists of.[35] All this is appropriate enough to the poetry of
the *trouvaille*, and it is really surprising that Stevens so
rarely sounds precious or mincing. Why does he so often
sound more like his own giant,[36] the same great muscular
power evident in the most delicately unfamiliar as in the
grandly executed gesture? Why is he so clearly at home
with his speech? The answer is simple but not to be
neglected: Stevens is fully American. "The Americans
are not British in sensibility," he noted.[37] The truth of
this is evident from the relation that has come to exist
between English and American poetry; it is quite clear
that the tables of affinity no longer apply, and the inter-
course between the two is very much what it might be as
between two literatures in different but mutually intelligible languages. Stevens was not, of course, indifferent to
English poetry; that is impossible to an American poet.
But it is equally difficult for a literate American to escape
the attractions of Paris, and that special sense of being at
home in French culture which history has as it were
forced on the American intellectual. We ought to remind
ourselves, if the need arises, of the prevalence of American
usage and place-names in Stevens' poems, and of his
insistence that reality is what you see finely and imagine
fully from where you are and as what you are; as, for
example, on an ordinary evening in New Haven. "The
gods of China are always Chinese," he says,[38] and it is
one of his leading ideas. When reality and imagination
are fused, the marriage happens in a specific place: in
Notes toward a Supreme Fiction he calls this place Catawba

"They married well because the marriage-place | Was what they loved" (*C.P.*, p. 401).

An earlier poet of this marriage-place was Whitman. Stevens writes of him in "Like Decorations in a Nigger Cemetery" (*C.P.*, pp. 150–58):

> In the far South the sun of autumn is passing
> Like Walt Whitman walking along a ruddy shore.
> He is singing and chanting the things that are part of
>   him,
> The worlds that were and will be, death and day.
> Nothing is final, he chants. No man shall see the end.
> His beard is of fire and his staff is a leaping flame.

One could not do better than quote Mr Morse's comment on the resemblance between Whitman and Stevens:

> They have in common that sense of place and that loneliness which is so often its complement, in their lives as much as in their poems. . . . The "slap-dash intensity", the "contrariness", and even "the sophistication" run like streams through their work. We have made too much of certain aspects of Stevens . . . and too little of the native element. I do not mean any sort of factitious Americanism; but I do mean a quality of mind, a sense of the world and of the character of the poet. Who else except Whitman, Randall Jarrell asks, would have thought of using language (and here he has in mind Whitman's use of French and his characteristic catalogues) in the way Whitman does? And I should answer, Wallace Stevens.[39]

This is a matter where English readers have perhaps a slight advantage. On the whole they are under important disadvantages arising from the cultural and linguistic differences, and their relatively short acquaintance with Stevens; but at least they can see that Stevens is a profoundly American, to them a very foreign, poet.

After the publication of *Harmonium* he wrote a few

more poems, including the famous and a little over-rated
"Sea Surface full of Clouds" (1924); but then he seems to
have produced little for several years, "the years in
which he was consolidating his position in the business
world."[40] His labour on the poems for *Harmonium* may
have seemed to take him to a sort of terminus; although
it was a first volume it covered the work of a good many
years, and came out when the poet had reached the age
when others are thinking about a collected edition. Nor
was there, in Stevens—at any rate until near the end of
his career—much of that forward drive into new fields
which is characteristic of some poets—of Yeats, for example. In this connexion Morse pertinently cites Stevens'
adage, "Thought tends to collect in pools";[41] during
these years the new pools were perhaps slowly forming,
many scattered pot-holes filling up simultaneously. New
poems began to appear in 1930, and in the following year
Knopf published the second edition of *Harmonium*, which
added fourteen and dropped three poems, making up the
collection as we now have it in the *Collected Poems* of 1954.

During the thirties Stevens wrote a good many brief
poems, collected in *Ideas of Order* (1935, 1936) or not
collected, and to be found in *Opus Posthumous*. In the
middle of the decade he worked on the long poem *Owl's
Clover* (1936), a work many admire but which Stevens
rejected from the *Collected Poems* as "rhetorical";[42] and on
The Man with the Blue Guitar, which was published in 1937
in the volume *The Man with the Blue Guitar & Other
Poems*. This volume included *Owl's Clover* in a revised
form.

From that time forward there can have been few
intervals in Stevens' work on poems short and long, and
on a form new to him, the public lecture. *Parts of a World*,
a substantial collection of shorter poems, came in 1942.
In the same year *Notes toward a Supreme Fiction* was published, and two years later *Esthétique du Mal*. Both poems
were included in the next large collection, *Transport to*

Summer (1947). Three years later came *The Auroras of Autumn*, including *A Primitive like an Orb*, which had been separately published in 1948. When *The Auroras of Autumn* appeared, Stevens was over seventy, and he had already resisted proposals for a collected edition on the ground that this seemed "final, and he was not quite ready to call things to a halt. Actually, his interest in poetry had never been greater."[43] When he did produce the *Collected Poems* for his seventy-fifth birthday in 1954, it was with an entirely new and magnificent section called *The Rock*; and there are poems in *Opus Posthumous*, written between 1950 and 1954, which deserved inclusion. Finally, there are about twenty poems, written too late for the collected edition, and these—some of them extremely important—are printed in *Opus Posthumous*. The bulk of his published prose was written between 1942 and the year of his death, and is included in *The Necessary Angel* (1951) and *Opus Posthumous*, which also has a selection of the *Adagia*, notebook aphorisms written between 1930 and 1955. All this prose is intimately related to the poetry.

The fifteen years of Stevens' life from sixty on had been prolific beyond all normal expectation; yet he was throughout this period in a position of high responsibility in the world of business. He did not retire from this at the statutory age of seventy; and he declined an invitation from Harvard University to be Charles Eliot Norton Professor for 1955–6 because "he felt that a year away from his office would make retirement inevitable." "There are several things," he said in explanation, "that are of the utmost interest to me from which I have had to turn away and if I have been able to reconcile myself to the necessity of doing this, it is all the easier to reconcile myself to the necessity of passing up the present opportunity."[44] He goes on to speak nobly of the need, which his occupation of so distinguished a professorship might have furthered, to enquire after a theory of poetry, "that would make poetry a significant humanity of such a nature and scope that it could be established as a normal, vital field of study for all comers." It is not altogether easy to understand the "necessity" which compelled him to spend his last years in business if he wanted to do something else. In 1940 he told Charles Henri Ford that as he was getting older he grew "more jealous of the demands business makes," and said, "I should like to devote more—all—of my time to the study and writing of poetry."[45] He was capable of remarking that he had "no life except in poetry"[46]—indeed this is the only view of the matter strictly consistent with his poems; yet he could also say, "Money is a kind of poetry."[47] Morse has this charitable comment:

> Later on he came to feel that too much had been made of his having pursued two careers successfully; and it is no exaggeration to say that his material success made it possible for him to sit still in order to discover the world, to indulge his imagination, and spend more and more time in "looking."[48]

Money can buy the right kind of leisure and the right kind of books and pictures; if they had the chance to try it, and found, as Stevens did, that the two vocations—money and poetry—could be combined, few poets, one supposes, would refuse the offer of Stevens' income on the same terms, even if the business was insurance. At the root of the animosity evidently felt towards Stevens for continuing in business there lies, I think, a simple acceptance of the myth that the poet has to be alienated, estranged from society, and that he ought to be defiant about it. Stevens was indeed fruitfully "different," but in a way that disappoints the myth. None of this would matter were it not that hostile commentators profess to find harmful effects in the poetry, arguing that Stevens dodged "life" not only in his vice-presidential office but in his poems, and that his poetry "has an air of sumptuousness, *chic*, expensiveness, 'conspicuous consumption': for work in his lines, only posh epithets need apply."[49] This attitude was perhaps encouraged by Stevens' manner during public appearances towards the end of his life, for he was, it seems, not easily approachable, not altogether on easy terms with his audiences; oracular in his manner, private in his dialect. Mary McCarthy was almost certainly thinking of Stevens when, in her novel *The Groves of Academe*, she described a distinguished visiting poet at a conference as "John D. Rockefeller drenched in attar of roses"—rich, affected, powerful, exotic. When the lecture "Imagination as Value" first appeared in print, I myself, knowing little of Stevens, wrote somewhat derisively of the lecture as belonging to what was apparently a "new American *genre*" and marvelled at the ability of an audience to be still understanding the lecture "at the point where one's aunt in California transmits that pregnant communication about her geraniums."[50] I now know not only that this is a work of the highest calibre, but also that I was wrong in supposing that anybody followed it at first hearing.

Mr Warner Berthoff of Bryn Mawr tells me, from his own experience, what a lecture by Stevens was like. The work in question was later to be called "Three Academic Pieces,"[51] which opens with a fully characteristic aphorism—"The accuracy of letters is an accuracy with respect to the structure of reality"—and proceeds to make certain points fundamental to Stevens' theory of poetry. These are not hard to take if you know the rest of Stevens, but must have been puzzling to the audience, particularly as the second half of the lecture was frankly a poem—called "Someone puts a Pineapple together"—and not a prose meditation with a poem's structure.

This performance was given at Harvard in 1947. "Everybody knew that this was a great occasion," says Mr Berthoff, "for it was known that he did not read in public (and hadn't been up to then much invited to) and he drew a big crowd." After the "Three Academic Pieces" he went on to read from his verse, but

nothing already in print, none of the old *Harmonium* familiars. After a while people began to leave—not so many really and mostly from the back of the big room—but enough to make some disturbance: shuffling, folding of chairs, gathering of coats and books, door squeaking, and so on. At this point he looked up, as slyly as was possible without in the least ruffling a very natural and unassuming dignity, and said that his next (or was it the last?) poem was called "As you leave the Room."[52] The poems referred to in it he had read earlier in the hour.[53] (I'm quite sure now that it was late January or early February, and there was indeed snow outside; it was a famous winter in Boston.) There was nothing to indicate that he hadn't composed it on the spot—perhaps he did. It was tremendously impressive—the whole reading, I mean.[54]

The poem "As you leave the Room" is a wonderful example of Stevens' late powers; apparently casual, fortuitous, it testifies to a maturity in which almost every utterance might make a memorable poem. But the first version of it is far less apt to Mr Berthoff's occasion—it does not mention snow—and only that version is early enough for Stevens to have used at Harvard. (The snow, incidentally, is less a matter of Boston than of Stevens' weather; he was probably thinking of the early poem called "The Snow Man" (*C.P.*, p. 9). But Mr Berthoff's memory has at least virtual truth. The poem has a Yeatsian quality—"those images that yet | Fresh images beget"—it is Stevens' "Circus Animal's Desertion," and, like some others among his later poetry, sounds, to borrow an expression used by John Wain in conversation on this topic, like "a fragment broken off the monolith of his own dialect."

There is also accuracy in the picture of turned backs

and squeaking doors. Stevens never tried to get on easy terms with a public; and fact coincides with myth to this degree, that he does seem to have kept his Hartford life clear of literary people. There is a story, told me by a very distinguished American writer, concerning an English philosopher of the greatest distinction, who met Stevens at a lecture in Harvard and asked if he might call at Hartford; the answer was a blunt and unqualified "No," with nothing to palliate the old man's discomfiture. Stevens was a very big, formidable man, though gentle in manner; he had obviously long assumed that one makes decisions and that these decisions then take effect. He had enforced that privacy which it was in his power to preserve, and which was the voluntary equivalent of the alienation regarded as necessary for other poets; but perhaps it was a condition to be maintained by a certain degree of egotism, perhaps it involved a few rather shocking gestures of this kind.

At the beginning of this chapter I discussed the manner in which some specific experience might intrude into Stevens' work. At the end of his life people and places came in on the same terms: Santayana in the great poem "To an Old Philosopher in Rome" (*C.P.*, pp. 508 ff.), the spring of New England in the lecture "Two or Three Ideas" (1951).[55] But the first is not only a tribute to an old master, it is a meditation on the "Profound poetry of the poor and of the dead." And the second is an occasion not only to celebrate the law of change, the fierce springs that pulse through all the poetry, but to speak with due solemnity of the part of poetry in the world:

Here in New England at this very moment nothing but good seems to be returning; and in that good, particularly if we ignore the difference between men and the natural world, how easy it is suddenly to believe in the poem as one has never believed in it before, suddenly to require of it a meaning beyond what its words can possibly say, a sound beyond any giving of the ear, a motion beyond our previous knowledge of feeling.[56]

When Stevens sees a bride being photographed in the park at Hartford, she becomes "the genius of poetry . . . out of place."[57] When he speaks of an unexpected friend, it is to explain the difference between what he calls a specialist and an all-round man; his young Korean friend was one of the latter. "He used to come up to Hartford and the two of us would go out to Elizabeth Park in Hartford, and sit on a bench by the pond and talk about poetry. He did not wait for the ducks to bring him ideas but always had in mind questions that disclosed his familiarity with the experience of poetry."[58] Watching these ducks became part of Stevens' experience of poetry, and perhaps this lake and these ducks are the ones in *Notes toward a Supreme Fiction*; but here they are specified, because of the chance that brought the young man, because he (like Stevens himself, one may gather from the preceding page) was something of an all-round man, unlike the philosophers of the East; like Horatio rather than Hamlet, illustrating the difference not only between those who meditate and those who act, but also—and here comes the voice of the big man who has given things up to get what he wants—"between the man who can talk about pictures and the man who can afford to buy them."

Mr G. S. Fraser, to show us how Stevens cut himself off from life, draws attention to two of the *Adagia*. The first says, "Life is an affair of people and not of places. But for me life is an affair of places and that is the trouble." The second: "Life is not people and scene but thought and feeling."[59] But the bleakness of these aphorisms is as illusory as their apparent contradictoriness. Immediately before the second of them occurs this adage: "Poets acquire humanity." No poet ever wrote so fixedly from within the human head as Stevens; for him "people and scene" might, at moments, appear to be nothing but a dangerous simplification of the human interest, a way of suggesting that reality is something more than the dry stick into which poetry infuses the sap.[60] Yet that life is an affair of places is true on the same supposition that poets are human; where they are is an important part of what they are: the gods of China are always Chinese. "The greatest poverty is not to live | In a physical world"[61] —and living in a physical world is living in a place. Or, to put it more obscurely:

> A scholar, in his Segmenta, left a note,
> As follows, "The Ruler of Reality,
> If more unreal than New Haven, is not
>
> A real ruler, but rules what is unreal."[62]

Morse ends *Opus Posthumous* with a piece called "Connecticut," written by Stevens in the last year of his life. "There are no foreigners in Connecticut," says Stevens. "It is a question of coming home to the American self in the sort of place in which it was formed. Going back to Connecticut is a return to an origin."[63] If our view of what might be American and true to the "origin of hardihood, good faith and good will" excludes the insurance lawyer who collected pictures and made, quite deliberately, a world in which truth and pleasure are inseparable, we shall have to revise it; for Stevens is an original American.

REFERENCES

1. In each case the first date is that of first publication by A. A. Knopf, New York; the second is the date of the first publication in Britain by Faber & Faber.

2. This account is particularly indebted to: Alfred Kreymborg, *Our Singing Strength* (1929), pp. 501 ff.; Harriet Monroe, *A Poet's Life* (1938); W. Van O'Connor, *The Shaping Spirit* (1950); S. F. Morse, Preface to *Opus Posthumous* (1957); and "The Native Element," *Kenyon Review*, xx (1958), 446 ff.;

René Taupin, *L'Influence du Symbolisme sur la Poésie Américaine* (1929); H. Simons, "Wallace Stevens and Mallarmé," *Modern Philology*, XLIII (1945–6), 235 ff.

3. "About one of Marianne Moore's Poems," *The Necessary Angel* (1951), pp. 99–101.

4. Memorandum addressed to Henry Church in 1940, Morse, Preface to *O.P.*, p. xiv.

5. *Adagia*, *O.P.*, p. 159. See also *Notes Toward a Supreme Fiction*, III. vii, *Collected Poems* (1954), p. 403.

6. *N.A.*, pp. 98–9.

7. *N.A.*, p. 102.

8. *N.A.*, p. 103.

9. "Another Weeping Woman," *C.P.*, p. 25.

10. Cf. *Adagia*, *O.P.*, p. 167, "Which is correct . . .".

11. *The Man with the Blue Guitar*, v, in *C.P.*, p. 167.

12. "A Thought Revolved," ii, in *C.P.*, p. 185.

13. Thirteen were printed in a Wallace Stevens number of the *Harvard Advocate* (December 1940). See O'Connor, *Shaping Spirit*, p. 14, and Morse, Preface to *O.P.*, p. xvii.

14. William Carlos Williams, quoted by O'Connor, *Shaping Spirit*, p. 15.

15. Morse, Preface to *O.P.*, p. xvii.

16. Morse, Preface to *O.P.*, p. xviii.

17. *O.P.*, pp. 3–6.

18. Harriet Monroe, *A Poet's Life*, pp. 342–3.

19. Monroe, p. 390.

20. Morse, Preface to *O.P.*, p. xxviii.

21. *O.P.*, p. 127.

22. *O.P.*, p. 10–16.

23. *Shaping Spirit*, p. 15.

24. *O.P.*, p. xxxix.

25. Letter to Kreymborg, quoted by O'Connor, *Shaping Spirit*, p. 10.

26. *Kora in Hell* (1920) quoted by O'Connor, p. 9.

27. Morse, Preface to *O.P.*, pp. xx–xxi.

28. Letter to Harriet Monroe, quoted by Morse, Preface to *O.P.*, p. xxi.

29. ibid.

30. Letter to W. C. Williams, quoted by Morse, "The Native Element," p. 452.

31. Quoted in Simons, "Wallace Stevens and Mallarmé," p. 235.

32. Simons, in his long and careful article, seems too laborious, too concerned with the manipulation of parallels; but he does succeed in relating Stevens' colour symbolism to that of Mallarmé. There seems little value in the attempt to limit the influence of Mallarmé to the years 1915–19. Of the parallel passages, the most convincing example is the resemblance between "Las de l'amer repos" and "Le Monocle de mon Oncle," vi, 1–3 (*C.P.*, p. 15).

33. Taupin, *L'Influence*, p. 276.

34. Preface to *O.P.*, pp. xxiv–xxv; *O.P.*, pp. 119–26.

35. e.g., *Shaping Spirit*, p. 135; Robert Pack, *Wallace Stevens* (1958), p. 183.

36. For the giant, see below, pp. 74 ff.

37. *Adagia, O.P.*, p. 176.

38. "Two or Three Ideas," *O.P.*, p. 211.

39. Morse, "The Native Element," p. 464.

40. Morse, "The Native Element," p. 457.

41. *Adagia, O.P.*, p. 170.

42. Morse, Preface to *O.P.*, p. xxiii.

43. Preface to *O.P.*, p. xiii.

44. Preface to *O.P.*, p. xvi.

45. "Verlaine in Hartford," *View*, 1 (1940) quoted by O'Connor, pp. 19–20.

46. *Adagia, O.P.*, p. 175.

47. *Adagia, O.P.*, p. 165.

48. Morse, "Native Element," p. 457.

49. G. S. Fraser reviewing *O.P.*, *New Statesman & Nation*, 9 Jan. 1960, pp. 43–4.

50. Review of *English Institute Essays 1948* (1949), *Review of English Studies*, N.S., II (1951), 96.

51. *N.A.*, pp. 71–89.

52. *O.P.*, pp. 116–17. And see the earlier version, "First Warmth," *O.P.*, pp. 89–90.

53. Notably "Someone puts a Pineapple Together," "The Well Dressed Man with a Beard," "A Primitive Like an Orb," "Credences of Summer," and possibly parts of "Examination of the Hero in a Time of War" (*C.P.*, pp. 247, 440 ff., 372 ff., and 296 ff.), and *N.S.F.* All these poems except the first and "A Primitive" were in fact published at the time of the lecture.

54. Letter to F.K., 25 Oct. 1958.

55. *O.P.*, pp. 202 ff.

56. *O.P.*, p. 210.

57. Speech at the ceremony for the award of the medal of the Poetry Society of America, 1951; *O.P.*, p. 242.

58. "The Whole Man: Perspectives, Horizons," *O.P.*, p. 231.

59. *Adagia, O.P.*, pp. 158, 170.

60. *Adagia, O.P.*, p. 171.

61. *Esthétique du Mal*, xv, *C.P.*, p. 325.

62. *An Ordinary Evening in New Haven*, xxvii, *C.P.*, p. 485.

63. "Connecticut," *O.P.*, p. 296.

CHAPTER II

HARMONIUM AND *IDEAS OF ORDER*

"The poem is a nature created by the poet,"[1] and all his poems, presided over by the same personality, make one great world. Stevens thought of his poetry as a world, which, to distinguish it from the "real" world, he called his *mundo*. "Pour le poète, comme pour Dieu, le parole devient monde," said his friend Jean Wahl;[2] and this world is created by the union of reality and the imagination; it is the world of what Stevens called the Supreme Fiction. Over the skeleton of reality the mind weaves its always changing, always delightful, fictive covering. "It is the *mundo* of the imagination in which the imaginative man delights and not the gaunt world of reason. The pleasure is the pleasure of powers that create a truth that cannot be arrived at by the reason alone, a truth that the poet recognizes by sensation."[3] This is not a rational world; it is, as Stevens puts it in a late poem, "the more than rational distortion, | The fiction that results from feeling."[4] By the time he wrote that, Stevens knew his world, its network of analogies, its fictive landscapes and fictive population, with an intimacy that made him both a more prolific and a more reflective poet. But it is the same world he first described in *Harmonium*: first the poems "Completely physical in a physical world," and later

> the thesis scrivened in delight,
> The reverberating psalm, the right chorale.[5]

First *Harmonium*, and later more of *Harmonium*, but with more rhetoric and more meditation. "One poem proves another and the whole."[6] Stevens wanted to call the collected edition of 1954 *The Whole of Harmonium*.[7]

This is a little too simple; *Harmonium* is not without its meditative poems, and it contains in the germ a great deal of what might be called the doctrine of Stevens, although the word suggests an assertiveness absent from his world. But it is true that *Harmonium* is on the whole very much more concerned than the later poetry with establishing the contours, the colours, the fortuity of Stevens' world—with reality "arranging itself into poems"[8] of the "gaudiness"[9] necessary to the fictive presentation of its own texture, its own strangeness. This is its theme, and it is a theme of delight. *Harmonium* has little—but not quite nothing—to say of what Stevens later came to call "poverty"—meaning the absence of a fruitful union between imagination and reality. Almost its only poverty is that of age and death, when the glitter dims and disappears, and the unexpected less often or never arranges itself into poems. That is a real impoverishment; and, like Coleridge his direct ancestor, Stevens is always conscious that the creative power may withdraw, that the time may come when one may see, without feeling, how beautiful the world is. But the main object of *Harmonium* is to be accurate, "to give a sense of the freshness or vividness of life,"[10] or, more completely, "The freshness of a world . . . the freshness of ourselves."[11] In the world of *Harmonium* the poet, young and virile, lives "in a kind of radiant and productive atmosphere. . . . The pleasure that the poet has there is a pleasure of agreement with the radiant and productive world in which he lives. It is an agreement that Mallarmé found in the sound of

Le vierge, le vivace et le bel aujourd'hui."[12]

Harmonium, then, is a volume of poems which live or die as physical objects radiating the freshness and pleasure of a transformed reality. They live; as one goes back to

C   W.S.

them again and again, having studied in Stevens' own school the physics of their world, the riches of *Harmonium* grow continually. It is a book of almost incredible gaiety, variety, and power; and it is a reminder that all the literary history in the world cannot predict the nature of a great poet. In one way and another *Harmonium* is of its age; but we perceive this either by hindsight, or in details which are not of the essence of the book.

It is true, for instance, that many of the short poems in *Harmonium* owe something to the ideals of Imagism, the catching of the exact curve of a thing, the rendering of what Hulme called the "intensive manifold," in rhythms untrammelled by conventional metre: brief insights into the physique of the world. Such poetry "always endeavours to arrest you, and to make you continuously see a physical thing, to prevent you gliding through an abstract process. It chooses fresh epithets and fresh metaphors, not so much because they are new, and we are tired of the old, but because the old cease to convey a physical thing and become abstract counters."[13] But although Stevens has this interest in the fresh and the concrete, although he—perhaps more than Pound, certainly more than Williams—has a mature virtuosity in the control of free verse rhythm, it is not easy to find a poem in *Harmonium* that does not, in the long run, invite the reader to "glide through an abstract process," if only to relate the individual case to the general law. *Harmonium* has, as Stevens insisted, "a single theme"—if only because, as is so often said, all the poems are "about poetry."

> In Oklahoma,
> Bonnie and Josie,
> Dressed in calico,
> Danced around a stump.
> They cried,
> "Ohoyaho,

Ohoo". . .
Celebrating the marriage
Of flesh and air.[14]

"Life," said Stevens later, "is a composite of the propositions about it."[15] Such a view is implicit in this little
poem with its fortuitous *locale*, its fictive characters
briefly endowed with life; they are dressed in a certain
way, and dance, like the poem, round a central stump.
But they would not be doing so if there existed no such
proposition as that implied in the last two lines. Life includes much nonsense,[16] some of it very gay—the gaiety
may sound hollow in so vast an arena, with so few props
—but these gauche figures, since they are dancing, make
their comment not on the loneliness or the poverty of
flesh in air, but on the joy that comes of the union of
men with the world.

In the same way, "Metaphors of a Magnifico" (*C.P.*,
p. 19) seems to be a celebration of what is irreducible in
the world of fact, the physical, the concrete:

Twenty men crossing a bridge,
Into a village,
Are twenty men crossing twenty bridges,
Into twenty villages,
Or one man
Crossing a single bridge into a village.

This is old song
That will not declare itself . . .

Twenty men crossing a bridge,
Into a village,
Are
Twenty men crossing a bridge
Into a village.

That will not declare itself
Yet is certain as meaning . . .

The boots of the men clump
On the boards of the bridge.
The first white wall of the village
Rises through fruit-trees.
Of what was it I was thinking?
So the meaning escapes.

The first white wall of the village . . .
The fruit-trees. . . .

This poem has the structure of an argument. What can
we make of the nursery-song opening? The first two
propositions (ll. 4–6) are unsatisfactory because we cannot understand the identity of each man by multiplying
bridge and village by twenty; and on the other hand the
men are different, and so not one man. We are left with
the tautology of ll. 9–13. All you can say for it is that it is
indisputable. But once we begin to supply the physical
reality—noise of boots, the wood of the bridge, a particular coloured wall, and some trees, the whole matter is
transformed. The philosophical problem is hereby
"evaded in the mind";[17] one is left with the physical
wall and the actual trees. . . . The difference between
this and a true Imagist poem is that the dismissal of the
abstract, the introduction of the victorious concrete, is
undertaken as a quasi-metaphysical task; the concrete is
defended in an abstract manner. In another poem[18]
Stevens urges the physical object, this time a star, to
"Shine alone . . . shine like fire, that mirrors nothing . . .
Lend no part to any humanity that suffuses | you in its
own light. Be not . . . half-man, half-star." This is a
genuine apostrophe to the object, urging it to remain free
of us, so that we may "see the earth again, | Cleared of
its stiff and stubborn, man-locked set";[19] it is not an
attempt "to convey a physical thing" but a prayer that
things should remain physical. So in "O Florida,
Venereal Soil" (*C.P.*, p. 47):

> A few things for themselves,
> Convolvulus and coral,
> Buzzards and live-moss,
> Tiestas from the keys,
> A few things for themselves,
> Florida, venereal soil,
> Disclose to the lover.

And, to sum it up:

> In my room, the world is beyond my understanding;
> But when I walk I see that it consists of three or four
>   hills and a cloud.[20]

Fact is important; without it we shall not achieve in poetry "a reality adequate to the profound necessities of life today."[21] But it is considered in relation to our need. It is the urgency of human need in respect of the thing— in itself, "the veritable *ding an sich*"[22] that provides a melancholy undertone to the gaiety of *Harmonium*; later it will be heard more clearly, when Stevens no longer even resembles an Imagist.

> From this the poem springs: that we live in a place
> That is not our own and, much more, not ourselves
> And hard it is in spite of blazoned days.[23]

Since *Harmonium* is the work of the poet's mature years, we should not expect it to show much evidence of un- assimilated influence. Just as Imagism is to Stevens a discipline interesting but not requiring submission, so the examples of Verlaine, of Mallarmé, of Laforgue, of the early Eliot, are studied and assimilated. There is, for example, a Ninetyish, even pre-Raphaelite tinge in these lines:

> She said, "My dear,
> Upon your altars,
> I have placed
> The marguerite and coquelicot,

And roses
Frail as April snow. . . ."[24]

But this is not a banal imitation; it belongs to the habit
of irony which underlies the affectations of Stevens'
manner. The mask of the poet is comic; hence the real
affinity with Laforgue, of which Stevens' *logopoeia*—to
use Pound's term—is one aspect. Mr Yvor Winters, who
dislikes "Laforguian irony," characterises it as the poetry
of the "double mood"; this passage, for instance, is suffi-
ciently like Stevens:

> Permettez, ô sirène,
> Voici que votre haleine
> Embaume la verveine;
> C'est le printemps qui s'amène !
> —Ce système, en effet, ramène le printemps,
> Avec son impudent cortège d'excitants.

Whether or no this represents "a vice of feeling"[25] is not
the present point, which is that irony of the Laforguian
type, together with many other mocking and self-
mocking devices, "an excess of alliteration which renders
the style perversely finical,"[26] a love for the strange or
unexpected word or for the unheard-of word, are all a
part of the comic *persona* of the *Harmonium* poet.

On Stevens' manner of addressing the world in *Harmonium* there is one study that deserves to be called classi-
cal: Mr R. P. Blackmur's essay, "Examples of Wallace
Stevens" (1931), which takes the poet's air of preciosity
as its starting-point. It arises from

such words as fubbed, girandoles, curlicues, catarrhs,
gobbet, diaphanes, clopping, minuscule, pipping,
pannicles, carked, ructive, rapey, cantilene, buffo,
fiscs, phylactery, princox, and funest. And such phrases
as "thrum with a proud douceur," or "A pool of pink,
clippered with lilies scudding the bright chromes,"
hastily read, merely increase the feeling of precious-

ness. Hence Mr Stevens has a bad reputation among those who dislike the finicky, and a high one, unfortunately, among those who value the ornamental sounds of words but who see no purpose in developing sound from sense.

Both classes of reader are wrong. Not a word listed above is used preciously; not one was chosen as an elegant substitute for a plain term; each, in its context, was a word definitely meant.[27]

Mr Blackmur makes good this claim in long and subtle analyses. The language of *Harmonium* is an *accurate* language, and "the accuracy of accurate letters is an accuracy with respect to the structure of reality." But nature is not a printing-press; it produces not identical things, but things that resemble one another. "Its prodigy is not identity but resemblance and its universe of reproduction is not an assembly line but an incessant creation. Because this is so in nature, it is so in metaphor."[28] The result, if you don't like it, is what Yvor Winters calls "a quest for the new, which, in the realm of emotion divorced from understanding or any principle of propriety, can be found only in new degrees of intensity and strangeness";[29] or, if you do like it, "something new which has the air of something condensed. This is the quality that makes his poems grow, rise in the mind like a tide."[30]

So far I have spoken only of free-verse poems. They are not, I think, his best, but in them one can best understand the firmness of his poetic plots (as in "Metaphors of a Magnifico" for example), the extraordinary delicacy of his rhythms, and that "infallible mastery of pause and tone" which, as Marianne Moore says, accompanies "a certain demureness of statement." (Even this is consistent with what she elsewhere calls his "bravura."[31]) Winters gives a very exact account of the rhythm of "The Snow Man,"[32] correctly emphasising its remarkable range and control, its integration in the emotional and metaphysical plots of the short poem. An example of more rigid rhythmic plotting is in "The Death of a Soldier" (*C.P.*, p. 97):

> Life contracts and death is expected,
> As in a season of autumn.
> The soldier falls.
>
> He does not become a three-days personage,
> Imposing his separation,
> Calling for pomp.
>
> Death is absolute and without memorial,
> As in a season of autumn,
> When the wind stops,
>
> When the wind stops and, over the heavens,
> The clouds go, nevertheless,
> In their direction.

This poem is syntactically direct; it makes a point. But the point is so qualified by irrational relations between one phrase and another—verbal repetition, rhythmic resemblance, unspoken associations of image—that it makes a very good example of that co-existence of precision and ambiguity in a single poem of which Mr Blackmur speaks.[33] The shrinking of human life with age, the approach of death, is like autumn (not only because we pass from ripeness to infertility and death, but because to do so is an acceptable condition of life). The dead soldier is not known about, therefore not set apart for reverence and a funeral; his death is (and all death ought to be) as final as the death of the year in autumn. But the repetition of this line is an illustration of how, in Stevens, the same is always changed when repeated; for in the second season of autumn the wind stops, as the soldier fell; it stops as he did but everything goes on, the clouds continue in the higher air, as life continues. There is no line which is not, on a second reading, qualified by some other line; precision breeds ambiguity. In some poems these connexions are made by rhyme also; it can be an instrument of "bravura" in comic instances like "barouche—Scaramouche," but it can be, either fitfully or by its very intrusiveness, an instrument of plot, as in the brilliant "Cortège for Rosenbloom" and "The Bird with the Coppery Keen Claws" and "The Man whose Pharynx was Bad" (*C.P.*, p. 96).

We may say of the innovations of rhythm and rhyme, as Mr Blackmur did of the "gaudy" language, that they are strange but always precise and accurate. Stevens is devotedly euphuistic, in the sense given to that word by his master Santayana.[34] "I have never been able to see why what is called Anglo-Saxon should have the right to higgle and haggle all over the page, contesting the right of other words," he said. "If a poem seems to require a hierophantic phrase, the phrase should pass."[35] And this defiance will serve also for rhyme and rhythm.

Winters, against his own principles, admired the subtleties of "The Snow Man"; but he also pointed out that Stevens was "perhaps the only living poet who has practised the new and the old meters simultaneously and at a high level of excellence."[36] He added that Stevens "in early maturity," had "a style which was the result of a fine native gift enriched by the study of English blank verse."[37] And a great many of the poems best known, and indeed best, in *Harmonium* are written in a blank verse as idiosyncratic, as rhythmically inexhaustible, as the language is full, coloured, and accurate. It has more than once been claimed (as by Marianne Moore) that these " 'noble accents and lucid, inescapable rhythms' point to the universal parent, Shakespeare."[38] It is another mark of Stevens' fundamental independence that these poems were written at a time when Mr Eliot was very busy with the argument that blank verse was no longer a viable form; Stevens simply makes it so, seeing that it is so, for him anyway. The wilder *bravura*, it is true, tends to occur in the free-verse poems, like "Ploughing on Sunday" (*C.P.*, p. 20), yet the celebrated "Bantams in Pine-Woods" (*C.P.*, p. 75)—"Chieftain Iffucan of Azcan in caftan | Of tan with henna hackles, halt!'"— has a regular blank-verse basis. But the unique long splendours of "Sunday Morning," "Le Monocle de mon Oncle," "On the Manner of addressing Clouds," "Of Heaven considered as a Tomb," "To the One of Fictive Music," "Anatomy of Monotony,"[39] are Stevens' irrefutable claim to a place in the tradition of meditative blank-verse writing.

It is the meditative element of *Harmonium* that reminds us most strongly of the unity of Stevens' world, for it grew stronger as the summer colours of the *mundo* grew dimmer. I shall return to the great poems, but I want now to show how pervasive in *Harmonium* are the themes and images which Stevens later identified as illustrating the laws of his world. These images and themes are here presented fairly systematically, though not of course exhaustively. The important thing for the reader of Stevens is to see the interlacing that binds the great early poems with the greater and different work of his old age.

For example, the seasons—not only as a natural analogue to the phases of human life but also as figuring the cyclical nature of the creative imagination—become dominant motives in the later work, and they are present, inexplicitly, in *Harmonium*. Out of "The Snow Man" (*C.P.*, p. 9) grows the recurring metaphor of winter as a pure abstracted reality, a bare icy outline purged clean of all the accretions brought by the human mind to make it possible for us to conceive of reality and live our lives. So purged, reality has no human meaning, nor has a man; he is

> . . . the listener who listens in the snow,
> And, nothing himself, beholds
> Nothing that is not there and the nothing that is.

In winter, things are seen as they are. Later, Stevens must have taken immediately to heart some words of Valéry in his dialogue *Dance and the Soul*, for which he wrote an admiring Introduction, almost his last prose:

> No doubt there is nothing more morbid in itself, more inimical to nature, than *to see things as they are*. . . . The real, in its pure state, stops the heart instantaneously. . . . O Socrates, the universe cannot for one instant endure to be only what it is. . . . The mistakes, the appearances, the play of the dioptrics of the mind deepen and quicken the world's miserable mass. . . . The idea introduces into what is, the leaven of what is not.[40]

The arrival of spring is the analogue of the mind's producing "what will suffice"[41] to clothe the intolerable body of reality. The "golden fury" with which spring "vanishes the scraps of winter," the passion with which

> Winter and spring, cold copulars, embrace
> And forth the particulars of rapture come,[42]

are hinted at in "Nomad Exquisite" (*C.P.*, p. 95):

> As the immense dew of Florida
> Brings forth
> The big-finned palm
> And green vine angering for life. . . .
>
> And blessed mornings,
> Meet for the eye of the young alligator,
> And lightning colors,
> So, in me, come flinging
> Forms, flames, and the flakes of flames.

The want of vitalising change is the theme of "Depression before Spring" (*C.P.*, p. 63). The superb poem called "The Man whose Pharynx was Bad" (*C.P.*, p. 96) had in its original version[43]—unaccountably mutilated in

Harmonium—a statement of the private significance of summer and winter, considered as satisfactory opposites, which compares well with anything in "Credences of Summer" and *Notes Toward a Supreme Fiction*. Summer is the season of the physical paradise, the full human satisfaction, when imagination for a moment as long as midsummer fully accounts for reality, makes it wholly bearable to human beings. But "The Man whose Pharynx was Bad" is Stevens' "Dejection Ode," a poem of intense feeling about the incapacity to feel even the greatest forces, to exert any imaginative pressure on reality:

> The time of year has grown indifferent.
> Mildew of summer and the deepening snow
> Are both alike in the routine I know.
> I am too dumbly in my being pent.
>
> The wind attendant on the solstices
> Blows on the shutters of the metropoles,
> Stirring no poet in his sleep, and tolls
> The grand ideas of the villages.
>
> The malady of the quotidian. . . .
> Perhaps if summer ever came to rest
> And lengthened, deepened, comforted, caressed
> Through days like oceans in obsidian
>
> Horizons, full of night's midsummer blaze;
> Perhaps, if winter once could penetrate
> Through all its purples to the final slate,
> Persisting bleakly in an icy haze,
>
> One might in turn become less diffident,
> Out of such mildew plucking neater mould
> And spouting new orations of the cold.
> One might. One might. But time will not relent.

This is very accurate: the wind of the solstices comes from the dead moments between seasons, the slack tide of imagination; it bears no news of the great world, only what is worn out, banal, quotidian. If it could be full summer or full winter (for "the absence of the imagination had | Itself to be imagined"[44]) this state of impotence might end. A related poem is "Banal Sojourn,"[45] where the discontent is a longing in the over-richness of high summer for the clean outline of winter. Cloyed with images, feeling the cyclical urge for change and purgation, the poet asks for winter:

> Moisture and heat have swollen the garden into
>   a slum of bloom.
> Pardie! Summer is like a fat beast, sleepy in
>   mildew,
> Our old bane, green and bloated, serene, who
>   cries,
> "That bliss of stars, that princox of evening
>   heaven!" reminding of seasons,
> When radiance came running down, slim
>   through the bareness.[46]

Perhaps we hear less of the mildew later; but the seasonal images are essentially present in *Harmonium*.

Another large and later much ramified theme so present is that of the Imagination. There are in the later Stevens many texts, prose and verse, on its power and our special need of it; Marius Bewley well says that "the Coleridgean imagination has become the theme of Stevens' poetry as a whole in a way it never became the theme of Coleridge's poetry as a whole."[47] It begins to be so in *Harmonium*.

In "Another Weeping Woman," (*C.P.*, p. 25) a poem about bereavement, there is a stanza which one might well have found in much later Stevens:

> The magnificent cause of being,
> The imagination, the one reality
> In this imagined world.

And "To the One of Fictive Music" (*C.P.*, p. 87) contains in little the substance of later poetry and prose meditations on the imaginative effort of the mind, especially in a time like the present when reality presses more imperiously, and the struggle to accommodate it to human needs is harder than ever before. This poem illustrates Stevens' power of sustained syntax—a power without which blank verse is a fallible instrument—and the first three stanzas are three highly complex, rapt, ornate sentences; it also uses rhyme. Its highly-wrought rhetoric is a warning against exaggerating the merely "physical" aspect of *Harmonium*. The human need of the saving fiction is stated in the last couplet:

> Unreal, give back to us what once you gave:
> The imagination that we spurned and crave.

The fictive power, which brings all the heaven there is to humanity, is affirmed more obliquely in the charming "Apostrophe to Vincentine," (*C.P.* p. 52) and with a tart fantastic euphoria in "A High-Toned Old Christian Woman" (*C.P.*, p. 59), which opens with a line that was to be the germ of Stevens' greatest poem: "Poetry is the supreme fiction, madame." The Woman is a widow; like "another weeping woman" she has allowed her imagination to go to Heaven with her husband, and needs to be told the truth.

> This will make widows wince. But fictive things
> Wink as they will. Wink most when widows wince.

Reality, in *Harmonium* as throughout Stevens, is that which the imagination, in different ways at different times and in different places, must contend with, compound with. He may represent it as a winter gauntness, or as the blue sky—"he would see things against the sky as a Christian would see them against the cross."[48] It is always that upon which the light of the mind must beat,

illuminating, warming, but not changing it. It matters
where you see it from:

> There are men whose words
> Are as natural sounds
> Of their places
> As the cackle of toucans
> In the place of toucans—[49]

and also, "I am what is around me."[50] It matters also
when one is looking; for the relation of the mind to reality
is always changing: "Let the place of the solitaires | Be
a place of perpetual undulation."[51] The fictions necessarily grow obsolete; "the plum survives its poems."[52]
Stevens has in mind, here as well as in the later poetry on
this topic, something like Bergson's *fonction fabulatrice*, a
mental power evolved to assist adaptation to the environment and ensure comfort and survival. Poets, with this
power, once made gods and myths, but these are irrelevant to modern reality. Now the same power must be our
defence against the poverty of fact. As early as "The
Ordinary Women" (*C.P.*, p. 10), the absence of imaginative happiness is called "poverty":

> Then from their poverty they rose,
> From dry catarrhs, and to guitars
> They flitted
> Through the palace walls.

The guitar is here, as in *The Man with the Blue Guitar*, an
emblem of the imagination, which "musicalises" reality.
The women live in a mythical palace of imagination; but
it grows stale and inadequate in its turn:

> Then from their poverty they rose,
> From dry guitars, and to catarrhs
> They flitted
> Through the palace walls.

So we may read back into *Harmonium* the laws, formulated later, of Stevens' *mundo*. It became more a matter for meditation,[53] but it remained the same world. It is merely that the inter-relations of its objects are more clearly seen, because more constantly dwelt upon; and some of them stand out more clearly from the colours and forms of the whole because they are recurrent topics of meditation. The candle which is the small light of the mind in "Final Soliloquy" (*C.P.*, p. 524) is the candle of *Harmonium*, which "burned alone in an immense valley."[54] The giant or hero of the later poems is the "Damned universal cock," the "ten-foot poet," of "Bantams in Pine-Woods" (*C.P.*, p. 75); the sea the giant lies beside in *Notes toward a Supreme Fiction* and *An Ordinary Evening in New Haven* (*C.P.*, pp. 387, 485) also confronts the "lacustrine" Calvinist in "The Doctor of Geneva" (*C.P.*, p. 24), and sets "his simmering mind"

> Spinning and hissing with oracular
> Notations of the wild, the ruinous waste.

In "Tea at the Palaz of Hoon" (*C.P.*, p. 65), the giant achieves his whole gigantic task almost as explicitly as twenty years later:

> Out of my mind the golden ointment rained,
> And my ears made the blowing hymns they heard.
> I was myself the compass of that sea:
>
> I was the world in which I walked, and what I saw
> Or heard or felt came not but from myself;
> And there I found myself more truly and more strange.

Since decay impairs, and death ends, the power of imagination over reality, one would expect even *Harmonium* to say something about them and it does; indeed it says more than might be expected in a work reputedly more concerned with objects and with texture than with persons. "God and the imagination are one";[55] *Har-*

monium acts on this assumption. Heaven is the work of the imagination, the light falling on reality and adding nothing but itself. Heaven therefore gutters and goes out.

Harmonium is not a young man's book; Stevens is out of the chamber of maiden thought. The flash and flare of its Florida, its paradise of earth, is known not merely in itself, but as part of a larger human whole which includes the idea of its loss. There are a number of extraordinary poems about death—the famous puzzle-piece, "The Emperor of Ice-Cream,"[56] "Cortège for Rosenbloom," "The Death of a Soldier," "The Jack-Rabbit," and, grandiloquently macabre, "The Worms at Heaven's Gate,"[57] which Taupin thought a "Parnassian" poem.[58] At the head of this class, at the head of the book, stands "Sunday Morning" (*C.P.*, p. 66). The great poem of growing old, of the sense of expiring sense, is "Le Monocle de mon Oncle" (*C.P.*, p. 13).

These two poems are of almost incomparable richness of rhythm and texture; but they are meditative poems, though "Le Monocle" is an altogether obscurer and more elusive meditation than "Sunday Morning." Both are famous, both have been written about almost too much.[59] The critic who praises "Sunday Morning" is rejoicing to concur in the sentiments of the common reader; and even Stevens' enemies continue with the Johnsonian encomium: had he often written thus it would be presumptuous to praise and useless to blame him. "Sunday Morning" is the hedonist's "Elegy in a Country Churchyard." We may say it illustrates two later *adagia*: "Wisdom asks nothing more"; and "After one has abandoned a belief in God, poetry is that essence which takes its place as life's redemption."[60] That leaves out everything. Into the reverie of the woman, free, accepting the sun and the colours of the world, comes the shadow of "ancient sacrifice," of "old catastrophe." Her dream translates her across the blankness of water "to silent Palestine, | Dominion of the blood and sepulchre."

D   W.S.

Why should she give her bounty to the dead?
What is divinity if it can come
Only in silent shadows and in dreams?
Shall she not find in comforts of the sun,
In pungent fruit and bright, green wings, or else
In any balm or beauty of the earth,
Things to be cherished like the thought of heaven?
Divinity must live within herself.

She must find it here. The creation of God was a mingling of what is human and what is beyond humanity. Shall that power to make a god fail us, or shall it make a human paradise on earth?

> . . . our blood, commingling, virginal,
> With heaven, brought such requital to desire
> The very hinds discerned it, in a star.
> Shall our blood fail? Or shall it come to be
> The blood of paradise? And shall the earth
> Seem all of paradise that we shall know?

If so, there will be no gulf between human and divine. But what, asks the lady, of death? The fourth stanza wonderfully dismisses the permanent elysia in favour of the paradise of transience; the fifth makes this transience, and therefore death, essential to paradise. "Death is the mother of beauty; hence from her, | Alone, shall come fulfilment to our dreams." Paradise without change is insipid, without desire, "unchanging, yet so like our perishing earth." The seventh stanza imagines the religion of the paradise of earth and death; the naked sun, stripped of its mythological attributes,[61] is celebrated as life-giver; the chant of the worshippers is "a chant of paradise, | Out of their blood, returning to the sky." They are "men that perish," and the dew on their feet is an emblem not of heavenly grace but of their earthly origin and destination. The lady knows that the tomb, empty of life, is only "the grave of Jesus, where he lay."

The wide water is not something to be crossed, but the preserver of our "island solitude," our world broken off from the sun, light and dark as the sun dictates. This is our condition; what are our joys?

> Deer walk upon our mountains, and the quail
> Whistle about us their spontaneous cries;
> Sweet berries ripen in the wilderness;
> And, in the isolation of the sky,
> At evening, casual flocks of pigeons make
> Ambiguous undulations as they sink,
> Downward to darkness, on extended wings.

In isolation this stanza has such quality that to call Stevens the greatest twentieth-century master of blank verse seems a tiresome understatement; but much of the wonder comes from the intimate firmness with which it is laced into the poem as a whole. The argument moves forward; the poem turns narcissistically in upon itself. The full force of some images emerges only years later, after prolonged meditation—the significance of birdsong, for example, in "Credences of Summer" and *Notes toward a Supreme Fiction*. Some of them are already fully "there" in the poem: the ripening berries and wilderness are specifically of an earthly, not a heavenly, paradise; the sky is isolated because we are bound for ever to our "island"; the birds move downward to darkness, but their movement is "ambiguous," full of the double meanings of human death; the wings, related by the passage in stanza four to a "desire for June and evening" are extended in the gesture of balance, in an environment with which they have a double relationship of control and surrender; the birds float down, making their fictive patterns as they go, into darkness.

The same metaphor occurs at the end of "Le Monocle de Mon Oncle," a poem with a more difficult argument but a hardly less enchanting text. There is here an element of the exquisite's self-parody which is lacking in

"Sunday Morning"; no one is clear about the title, and some other parts too.[62] The person addressed in the grand apostrophe of the opening is obviously not the uncle's wife, but, as far as she can be pinned down, "The One of Fictive Music" of the imagination ("And for what, except for you, do I feel love?"[63]). At forty, the man's memory recalls this Venus as radiant, and then as more than merely that. But his spring is past; he will join no choir of its celebrants, however persistently his mind, his interior lover, may remember such performances in the past. They, like the art of the hairdresser, were ephemeral. (This is the gist of st. iii; its last two lines are among the most beautiful in Stevens, and I do not know what they mean.) The fourth stanza (on which see Blackmur's comment[64]) relates life to ripeness in fruit, and develops the trope; life ripens and falls like an apple, and the apple has other symbolic meanings; as the forbidden fruit, it serves, like Yorick's skull, for the purposes of moralising on life and death; like the skull, it rots back to the ground. It is indeed a better emblem than the skull, in that it was also the cause of unreasonable passion, and comes to be moralised only when the moralist is too old to be passionate. Youth as the time of intense love, "measure . . . of the verve of earth," gives way to acquiescence in change; the firefly is a reminder of transience, as, long ago, one found in the noise of crickets a hint of mortality. At forty we are of the same substance as before; but the colours have settled down, the blues no longer vary (blue is, in Stevens' colour-system, for imagination) and the old amorous, delighted discriminations are dead. We may imagine an unearthly beauty, without the immediacy and vitality of our own, the one we have lost; but the second is certain, though it as certainly departs; the first "may or may not come" and the "eternal bloom" of the last line of vii is a paradox; reality knows no such thing. St. viii develops the parallel between the fruit and the man; battered, swollen, made grotesque by age, they finally die. He ironically calls (st. ix) for the special powers needed to "celebrate | The faith of forty." But he finds no unearthly inspiration, nothing that does not belong to decay; only the permanence of the tree to which all birds come suggests a human grasp of reality: of the plum that survives its poems, and the necessary passion of the young. But in our relation to reality we do more than produce the necessary noises of acquiescence; we produce the excess which is love or art. Finally, as the pigeons flutter to earth, their necessary downward movement produces distinct images; the mellowness of forty's wisdom brings one this knowledge, that the flicker of distinct, ephemeral images is the truth about life and love on the way to death.[65]

It is painful, but I hope useful, to mangle this great and obscure poem; it may well be an inaccurate account that is here offered, but with such verses it is true that one needs to quiet the housedog of the mind with any meat so that the poem may do its work.

One more *Harmonium* poem requires some mention, the long and difficult "Comedian as the Letter C" (*C.P.*, pp. 27–46). This is in every sense a fantastic performance: it is a narrative of obscurely allegorical intent, harsh and dream-like; and its manner is a sustained nightmare of unexpected diction, so that one sometimes thinks of it less as a poem than as a remarkable physical feat. The first section, "The World without Imagination," opens on a just tolerably familiar note:

> Nota: man is the intelligence of his soil,
> The sovereign ghost. As such, the Socrates
> Of snails, musician of pears, principium
> And lex. Sed quaeritur: is this same wig
> Of things, this nincompated pedagogue,
> Preceptor to the sea?

Crispin is given a fool's dialect; his learning is the learning of Feste. This means: man being the only creature of intelligence, spiritually endowed, is mind and soul of his world; he provides its *rationale* and its rules. But is this top creature, this clownishly endowed intellect, in the same position with respect to the sea? The sea, as usual, does not make human sense; porpoises are less intelligible than apricots. For all his terrestrial powers, Crispin makes nothing of the sea.

> What word split up in clickering syllables
> And storming under multitudinous tones
> Was name for this short-shanks in all that brunt?
> Crispin was washed away by magnitude.

Crispin here becomes, on his travels, "merest minuscule," the letter c, in fact. He "became an introspective voyager." " . . . The last distortion of romance | Forsook the insatiable egotist . . . Here was no help before reality."

> The imagination here could not evade,
> In poems of plums, the strict austerity
> Of one vast, subjugating, final tone.

In Sect. ii, "Concerning the Thunderstorms of Yucatan," the chastened Crispin passes into a landscape of "savage color." No longer sentimental about Nature and the seasons, he "found his vicissitudes had much enlarged | His apprehension," and

> perceived
> That coolness for his heat came suddenly,
> And only, in the fables that he scrawled
> With his own quill, in its indigenous dew,
> Of an aesthetic tough, diverse, untamed,
> Incredible to prudes, the mint of dirt,
> Green barbarism turning paradigm. . . .
> The fabulous and its intrinsic verse
> Came like two spirits parleying. . . .

We move into the tropical world, fat vegetation, rank fabling, a world "with new reality in parrot-squawks."

But Crispin takes shelter from the thunder in a cathedral. There is something harsher yet to learn.

This is not autobiography in fancy-dress, but steps toward the necessary relation with reality. The sea cures Crispin of his feebler imaginative habits; the experience of Yucatan brings a more mature operation of the *fonction fabulatrice*. But the green of Yucatan misses something out; and Crispin, "fagot in the lunar fire"—for the moon dominates imagination as the sun reality—returns to North America. The title of sect. iii is "Approaching Carolina," but even Carolina is the North, the cold, the sharp outline. "How many poems he denied himself | .... lesser things | Than the relentless contact he desired!" "The Arctic moonlight" provides a fuller liaison between him and his environment; but this was only "a minor meeting," and Crispin begins to travel between sun and moon (imagination and reality). Arriving in Carolina in spring—an unsuitable moment for one in search of "the fecund minimum"—he nevertheless learns "how much | Of what he saw he never saw at all." And he grips "the essential prose," the basic reality, still to be discovered, and underlying all poems. Now, at the beginning of sect. iv, the opening proposition of the poem can be corrected: "Nota: his soil is man's intelligence. | That's better." (This means, not, as Winters thought, that "he is bent on discovering the reality of his own country,"[66] i.e., America, but that order is to be discovered in the world, not imposed upon it by the human mind.[67] Certainly order depends upon where you discover it: "The natives of the rain are rainy men," "The Gods of China are always Chinese.") And at this point Stevens does, surely with intention, speak accurately of *Harmonium*:

> Hence the reverberations in the words
> Of his first central hymns, the celebrants
> Of rankest trivia, tests of the strength
> Of his aesthetic, his philosophy. . . .

Now Crispin defers to the world's fortuity, as Stevens did:
"Preferring text to gloss, he humbly served | Grotesque
apprenticeship to chance event." In sect. v he settles in a
"Nice Shady Home," a hermit and a planter. (The
planter figure recurs in *Notes toward a Supreme Fiction*, II.
v.) None of this means, as Winters supposes, that the
poet gets beyond writing poetry and ought either to give
up or change his ideas. It must be recognised—the same
recognition is enacted in the late "Bouquet of Roses in
Sunlight" (*C.P.*, p. 430)—that "The plum survives its
poems." To ignore this is to falsify reality. Crispin may have
reduced his aspirations; but "for realist, what is is what
should be." This is also a matter of growing old; for
Crispin at forty, perhaps, there is a mingling of ephemeral
blues into "basic slate." Out of this "quotidian" reality,
given love, there comes not poverty but "a humped
return," riches. Finally in sect. vi ("And Daughters with
Curls") Crispin has four daughters, "Infants yet emin-
ently old." He is living in the world, in his own place;
his daughters are, I think, without doubt the seasons,
cardinal to the life of Nature and his own life. And this
resolution, to live in the world, to let turnips be turnips
whatever he may produce in the way of comment and
enhancement, is the point where Crispin is clearly once
more Stevens. After *Harmonium* his poems, obviously, will
be different; "beginning with green brag, | Concluding
fadedly" perhaps; or distorting, "proving what he proves
| Is nothing." "What can all this matter," asks Stevens,
—for here, evidently, he was genuinely indifferent—
"since | The relation comes, benignly, to its end?" The
writing of this fantastic poem, the revising of it for publication in *Harmonium*, was not only a matter of confronting
poetry with reality; it was a way of ending the period which
might, though only with comic distortion, be called that
of "green brag." It was a long poem; perhaps the future
would hold many such. At any rate, *Harmonium* was over,
and changes might be expected.

On the changes that came over Stevens after *Harmonium* there are violent critical differences; and these ought to be explained. One may do this by citing the hostile—here represented by Yvor Winters and Randall Jarrell—and the friendly. Winters' essay, though deeply erroneous, is the classic statement of the case against Stevens; just as you need to have an answer for Dr Johnson if you profess to admire *Lycidas*, so you need to deal with Winters if you claim that Stevens wrote even better verse after "Sunday Morning."

The burden of Winters' critique is that Stevens declined rapidly, and betrayed his great gifts; he has a profound admiration for some poems in *Harmonium*, especially for "Sunday Morning," but thinks that the causes of the collapse can be observed even in that poem. It recommends "the cultivation of the emotions as an end in itself," which is the hedonism Winters castigates; he finds in it the explanation of Stevens' "rapid and tragic decay." Stevens, like Poe, declines to make poems which are "exercises in just feeling" and so "acts of moral judgment"; he is bent "on a quest for the new, which, in the realm of emotion divorced from understanding or any principle of propriety, can be found only in new degrees of intensity and strangeness." This "search is equally devoid of hope and of significance." "The Comedian as the Letter C" is a meditation on the obvious choice confronting Stevens: to go on with something hopeless, or to stop. Winters is sorry he went on.

There appears to be in the best of the early poems . . . a traditional rhetoric cognate with that attitude and precisely expressive of it. This traditional element in the early work enables Stevens' talent to function at its highest power; but it is not only unjustified and unsupported by Stevens' explicit philosophy, it is at odds with that philosophy. And the conflict between the traditional element and the element encouraged by the philosophy results little by little in the destruction of the traditional element and the degradation of the poet's style.[68]

Winters, writing in the early forties and before *Notes toward a Supreme Fiction*, is profoundly serious, and regards Stevens merely as a symptom of certain desperate ills he diagnoses in modern literature, sicknesses of form and substance. Stevens' hedonism brings its own punishment; triviality, false novelty, the collapse of a style.[69] I believe myself that the world of Stevens has an order, that in his novelties and his repetitions (which he himself clearly regards as important) there is precisely that fruitful relationship between the unique case and the general law that Winters declares to be absent; and that the order is ultimately a moral order. But it is "tough, diverse, untamed, | Incredible to prudes"—if one can say so without calling Stevens a solipsist or Winters a narrow moralist. I think we have here an example of incompatibility between two strong minds; and all Winters' evidence that Stevens is on a kind of primrose path can be used to illustrate the poet's fruitful restlessness in his own world, his determination to regard no armistice in "the war between the mind and sky" as a final treaty. We ought to remember that Winters was writing in the middle of what looked like one of Stevens' dry spells; I do not know if he has modified his view. I should guess not.

Mr Jarrell is a very different but still formidable opponent; he is certainly one of the most brilliant reviewers of poetry in our time. He loves *Harmonium* for reasons I won't go into, though they are novel; but finds that "the habit of philosophizing in poetry—or of seeming to philosophize, of using a philosophical tone, images, constructions, of having quasi-philosophical daydreams —has been unfortunate for Stevens."[70] (Jarrell seems to think that this tone, these images and constructions, were

absent from *Harmonium*.) He finds it symptomatic that
Stevens says of the Supreme Fiction "it must be abstract,"
ignoring the limited meaning Stevens gives to this word.[71]
(The poet "denies that abstraction is a vice | Except to
the fatuous.") "Surely a poet *has* to treat the concrete as
primary"—but Stevens always did, though he is also
interested in the possibilities for poetry of meditation on
why this should be so. "The real is only the base. But it is
the base."[72] There are later poems, it would be pointless
to deny, in which the dog is forgotten and the "canoid
patch" takes its place; it is true that in *Harmonium* more
than in the later poems "reality keeps breaking in." It is
true also that Stevens grows more and more Words-
worthian, in the sense that he cultivates the "egotistical
sublime" (a mode that can be "divinely void of pride"[73])
instead of "the chameleon's shameless interest in everything but itself." "The green spectacles show us a world
of green spectacles," says Jarrell. Without at all claiming
that there is not a higher proportion of failure in Stevens'
post-*Harmonium* poetry, one may say that Mr Jarrell's
kind of criticism, for all its skill and power, seems to work
only for the chameleontic sublime, and that he must
therefore miss much of the effect even of poetry he ad-
mires, like Yeats'. There is a poetry of the abstract; if you
do not like it, even when it is firmly rooted in the particulars of the world, you will not like Stevens.

What I take to be a fuller and more rewarding view of
the matter is expressed by Marius Bewley, who admits
that Stevens "allowed too many practice poems to
appear," especially in *Parts of a World*, but stresses the
interlacing between old and new poems in the Stevens
world, and deplores the "persistent bias in favour of
Stevens' first volume" which "has led to an underesti-
mation of the importance of meaning in his work as a
whole."[74] Meaning, Bewley believes, "has been consis-
tently developing from *Harmonium* towards the maturity
of the late work," and *Notes toward a Supreme Fiction* is

"Possibly . . . Stevens' greatest achievement." This view I entirely endorse. It is given fuller expression in an essay by Roy Harvey Pearce.[75]

> If the movement in the poems has been away from the descriptive and dramatic towards the discursive and dialectical, this is part of an immanent necessity rising out of a fixed subject-matter and the poet's steadily maturing view of it. Essentially, the styles of *Harmonium* and *Transport to Summer* [the latest volume at the time when Mr Pearce was writing] represent two modes of knowing. But the conception of the act of knowing, of the relation of the imagined to the real, remains constant. It is the degree of knowing, the complexity and inclusiveness of the knowledge, which grows. And it comes finally, in the major poems of *Transport to Summer*, to make for the possibility of mature, considered belief in the reality which we have "as and where we are."

Mr Pearce's valuable essay is evidence that the reward for understanding Stevens, for patience and persistence in a world that is devious and unexpected but at the same time self-consistent, is greater than the satisfaction of attacking him from the strong-point of a critical presumption, even if it is as well-built as Winters', or has the fire-power of Jarrell's. At any rate, we ought not to waste our time lamenting that the later volumes are not the same as *Harmonium*.

Ideas of Order, a volume of thirty-six poems, was Stevens' first new book for twelve years (if we except the second edition of *Harmonium*). The changes are perhaps less striking than one might have supposed. Stevens is writing, in his own phrase, as an "exponent of the imagination,"[76] as a student of its relation to reality. This does not in itself constitute a difference. Certain poems— "Dance of the Macabre Mice," "Meditation Celestial

and Terrestrial," "Lions in Sweden," "Some Friends
from Pascagoula," to mention four that occur within
half a dozen pages[77]—would be perfectly in place in
Harmonium. But the elegiac tone of "Le Monocle de Mon
Oncle" is heard more persistently, as in the splendid short
poem "The Sun this March" (*C.P.*, p. 133):

> The exceeding brightness of this early sun
> Makes me conceive how dark I have become. . . .
>
> Cold is our element and winter's air
> Brings voices as of lions coming down.
>
> Oh! Rabbi, rabbi, fend my soul for me
> And true savant of this dark nature be.

Again, in "Anglais Mort à Florence" (*C.P.*, p. 148): "A
little less returned for him each spring. . . . His spirit
grew uncertain of delight, | Certain of its uncertainty."
The world takes a sober colouring from his eye; he finds
in music hints of order, but the mood is not quite that of
Wordsworth finding strength in what remains behind:

> . . . he remembered the time when he stood alone.
>
> He stood at last by God's help and the police;
> But he remembered the time when he stood alone.
> He yielded himself to that single majesty;
>
> But he remembered the time when he stood alone,
> When to be and delight to be seemed to be one,
> Before the colors deepened and grew small.

This is a masterly poem, not at all famous, yet a perfect
example of Stevens' way of intoning the Romantic regret
in a voice chastened by irony. The loss is real; but it is
part of the whole human condition with which poetry
has to do (in a sense the loss would be greater if no such
loss occurred) and it is in itself a proper subject for
poetry:

Can all men together avenge
One of the leaves that have fallen in autumn?
But the wise man avenges by building his city in snow.[78]

At any rate the lines I have quoted from these poems (and see also the beautiful "Postcard from the Volcano," *C.P.*, p. 158) are all the evidence needed to show the quality of the art brought to this theme in *Ideas of Order*. This is the first step—or rather the second, for the first was taken in *Harmonium* itself—whereby the poet "by a deliberate process of self-knowledge, rebuild[s] himself and his poetry, rebuild[s] himself through his poetry,"[79] to achieve the great meditations of his last years. "It is not a question of setting up divisions, but of watching recessive elements in the early poetry develop into dominance." "If in the minds of men," says Stevens in the lecture "Two or Three Ideas,"[80]

creativeness was the same thing as creation in the natural world, if a spiritual planet matched the sun, or if without any question of a spiritual planet, the light and warmth of spring revitalized all our faculties, as in a measure they do, all the bearings one takes, all the propositions one formulates would be within the scope of that particular domination. The trouble is, however, that men in general do not create in light and warmth alone. They create in darkness and coldness.

Dealing with the dark and the cold, as well as with the light and warmth of the earth, a poet, or any man of imagination, may be led into evil or into a more inclusive good. It is a situation of some disquiet, and it is present in *Ideas of Order*; it calls not for renunciation but for poetry:

Chant, O ye faithful, in your paths
The poem of long celestial death;

For who could tolerate the earth
Without that poem?[81]

The "old chaos of the sun" now takes on a new, colder aspect, imaginatively matched and subdued in poems which could not have found a place in *Harmonium*. Here is one of them, "The Reader" (*C.P.*, p. 146); it will scarcely be regarded as inferior, but it is different:

> All night I sat reading a book,
> Sat reading as if in a book
> Of sombre pages.
>
> It was autumn and falling stars
> Covered the shrivelled forms
> Crouched in the moonlight.
>
> No lamp was burning as I read,
> A voice was mumbling, "Everything
> Falls back to coldness,
>
> Even the musky muscadines,
> The melons, the vermilion pears
> Of the leafless garden."
>
> The sombre pages bore no print
> Except the trace of burning stars
> In the frosty heaven.

Nevertheless, "ideas of order" must include the muscadine and the pear themselves as well as the idea of their fall back to coldness. When the volume was published in 1935 it opened with "Sailing after Lunch" (*C.P.*, p. 120), which, as Martz says, is "a curiously fatigued poem." But in the trade edition of 1936 the first poem is a new one, "Farewell to Florida" (*C.P.*, p. 117) in which Stevens "renounces all that 'Florida' had symbolized in his earlier poetry,"[82] but with a sort of elation that marks total acceptance. "I am free," he says, "Her mind had bound me round."

> How content I shall be in the North to which I sail
> And to feel sure and forget the bleaching sand. . . .

> To stand here on the deck in the dark and say
> Farewell and to know that that land is forever gone
> And that she will not follow in any word
> Or look, nor ever again except in thought, except
> That I loved her once . . . Farewell. Go on, high ship.

The raw personality of this poem gains so much from the
context of the *Collected Works*, that mass of qualified,
ironic, finished poetry, that it seems there to be a better
poem than it looks in isolation. It is not the last time
Stevens will brood on his own past, his own images; but
it has a special value, as if Gray had spoken out. Recog-
nising a need, it speaks of the conditions under which
the need might still be satisfied. This need, in fact, grows
even greater:

> The epic of disbelief
> Blares oftener and soon, will soon be constant.
> Some harmonious skeptic soon in a skeptical music
> Will unite these figures of men and their shapes
> Will glisten again with motion.[83]

The bigger poems of *Ideas of Order* are "Academic Dis-
course at Havana" (*C.P.*, p. 142), one of the failures, I
think, "Evening Without Angels" (*C.P.*, p. 136), and
"The Idea of Order at Key West" (*C.P.*, p. 128). "Evening Without Angels" is a meditation in the descent of
"Sunday Morning," though it looks forward to *Notes
toward a Supreme Fiction*:

> Was the sun concoct for angels or for men?
> Sad men made angels of the sun, and of
> The moon they made their own attendant ghosts,
> Which led them back to angels, after death.

It is the hedonist against the most hostile environment;
men, separated from the sky by the roofs of their houses,
against the naked dark:

> Bare night is best. Bare earth is best. Bare, bare,
> Except for our own houses, huddled low

Beneath the arches and their spangled air,
Beneath the rhapsodies of fire and fire,
Where the voice that is in as makes a true response,
Where the voice that is great within us rises up,
As we stand gazing at the rounded moon.

But "The Idea of Order at Key West" is the crown of the
volume, its "Sunday Morning." It is, as meditation, relatively simple to follow, but it quietly breeds its own richness
of internal reference. There is a singer and a sea; the sea
is Crispin's, "making faint memorial gesturings, | That
were like arms and shoulders in the waves," sounds hal-
lucinatingly human, what seems a sunken voice. The sea
is reality. But what the girl sang was not the sea, but
words; "it was she and not the sea we heard."

> For she was the maker of the song she sang.
> The ever-hooded, tragic-gestured sea
> Was merely a place by which she walked to sing.

This is the problem of imagination and reality. But the
"spiritual planet" does not "match the sun," and the
song was different from, more than, the water; finally it
imposed its order on the whole of reality.

> She was the single artificer of the world
> In which she sang. And when she sang, the sea,
> Whatever self it had, became the self
> That was her song, for she was the maker. Then we,
> As we beheld her striding there alone,
> Knew that there never was a world for her
> Except the one she sang, and, singing, made.

This is the sea of Florida, the sea of Crispin, caught up
into an order. As the two men return to the town they
see that its lights, human artifacts, have imposed an
order on the night, "Mastered the night and portioned
out the sea . . . Arranging, deepening, enchanting night."
This is the product of human need and the human imagination, the "blessed rage for order."

Such a poem may stand as a great, perhaps belated, climax to a whole age of poetry that begins with Coleridge and Wordsworth; it celebrates the power of the mind over what they called "a universe of death." It will be a poem that means something so long as we have any kind of belief in the lamp which Coleridge substituted for the mirror of Locke. We receive but what we give. One sees as belonging to a great family certain Romantic emblems, early and late: Wordsworth beside the pool bare to the eye of heaven and Yeats in the schoolroom; Mallarmé's lucky constellation swinging up over a marine chaos, and Stevens hearing his singer by the sea, deriding his angel, or contemplating the rock on which the lilacs grow and bloom like a blindness cleaned. It is those who cannot value the great founders of the tradition—and we should add the name of Blake, for Stevens is a bit like an agnostic Blake, too—who stick at *Harmonium* and do not see how such ideas of order can make poetry.

REFERENCES

1. *Adagia*, *O.P.*, p. 166.
2. *Poésie, Pensée, Perception*, (1948), p. 23.
3. "F.Y.V.P.," *N.A.*, p. 58.
4. *N.S.F.*, iii. x, *C.P.*, p. 406.
5. *Esthétique du Mal*, xv, *C.P.*, pp. 325–6.
6. "A Primitive like an Orb," *C.P.*, p. 441.
7. S. F. Morse, Preface to *O.P.*, p. xiv.
8. *Adagia*, *O.P.*, p. 165.
9. "The essential gaudiness of poetry" is Stevens' expression. Note in *Fifty Poets*, ed. W. R. Benèt, (1935), p. 46; quoted by O'Connor, *Shaping Spirit*, p. 43. There is a splendid development of the idea in Marianne Moore, *Predilections*, pp. 34–5.
10. *Adagia*, *O.P.*, p. 157. And for "accurate," see *Adagia*, p. 158 and "Three Academic Pieces," *N.A.*, p. 71.
11. *N.S.F.*, ii. x, *C.P.*, p. 398.
12. "F.Y.V.P.," *N.A.*, p. 57.
13. T. E. Hulme, *Speculations* (1924), p. 134.
14. "Life is Motion," *C.P.*, p. 83.
15. *Adagia*, *O.P.*, p. 171.
16. cf. *N.S.F.*, i. iii, *C.P.*, p. 383.

17. *N.S.F.*, I. ix, *C.P.*, p. 388.

18. "Nuances of a Theme by Williams," *C.P.*, p. 18.

19. "Angel Surrounded by Paysans," *C.P.*, p. 496–7.

20. "Of the Surface of Things," *C.P.*, p. 57.

21. "About one of Marianne Moore's Poems," *N.A.*, p. 102.

22. "The Comedian as the Letter C," *C.P.*, p. 29.

23. *N.S.F.*, I. iv, *C.P.*, p. 383.

24. "Cy est Pourtraicte, Madame Ste Ursule, et les Unze Mille Vierges," *C.P.*, p. 21.

25. Yvor Winters, "Wallace Stevens, or The Hedonist's Progress," *In Defense of Reason* (1947), pp. 65–6, 88.

26. Winters, p. 457.

27. "Examples of Wallace Stevens," in *Language as Gesture* (1952), reprinted in *Form and Value in Modern Poetry* (1957), pp. 183 ff.

28. "Three Academic Pieces," *N.A.*, pp. 71–3.

29. Winters, "Wallace Stevens," p. 439.

30. Blackmur, "Examples of Wallace Stevens," pp. 197–8.

31. M. Moore, *Predilections* (1956), pp. 46, 33.

32. *C.P.*, p. 9; Winters, *In Defense of Reason*, pp. 126–7.

33. "Examples of Wallace Stevens," p. 189.

34. Euphuism: "the choice of coloured words and rare elliptical phrases," see Santayana, *Interpretations of Poetry and Religion* (1900), Ch. X.

35. "Two or Three Ideas," *O.P.*, p. 205.

36. *In Defense of Reason*, p. 105.

37. *In Defense of Reason*, p. 433.

38. *Predilections*, p. 33.

39. *C.P.*, pp. 66 ff., 13 ff., 55–6, 56, 87–8, 107–8.

40. *L'Ame et la Danse* (1921), translated by W. McC. Stewart, in *Collected Works of Paul Valéry*, ed. Jackson Mathews, iv (1958), 51–2. Stevens' Prefaces to this volume were written early in 1955.

41. "Of Modern Poetry," *C.P.*, pp. 239–40; and associated poems in *Parts of a World*. See Ch. III below.

42. *N.S.F.*, II. ii, *C.P.*, p. 392.

43. Winters, "Wallace Stevens," pp. 437–8, gives the original version with a commentary emphasising its importance but misunderstanding the imagery.

44. "The Plain Sense of Things," *C.P.*, p. 503.

45. *C.P.*, pp. 62–3. For the idea of necessary change, closely related to the imagery of seasons, see also "The Place of the Solitaires," "The Curtains in the House of the Metaphysician," and "The Wind Shifts" (*C.P.*, pp. 60, 62, 83).

46. Cf. "Anatomy of Monotony," *C.P.*, pp. 107 ff.

47. M. Bewley, *The Complex Fate* (1952), p. 184.

48. Blackmur, "Examples of Wallace Stevens," p. 203.

49. "Anecdote of Men by the Thousand," *C.P.*, pp. 51–2.

50. "Theory," *C.P.*, p. 86.

51. "The Place of the Solitaires," *C.P.*, p. 60.

52. "The Comedian as the Letter C," *C.P.*, p. 41.

53. See "The World as Meditation," *C.P.*, pp. 520–1.

54. "Valley Candle," *C.P.*, p. 51. See also "Poem with Rhythms," *C.P.*, p. 245, and "A Quiet Normal Life," *C.P.*, p. 523.

55. "Final Soliloquy of the Interior Paramour," *C.P.*, p. 524.

56. *C.P.*, p. 64. Frequently explicated, several times by Stevens himself (see Morse, "The Native Element," p. 461). See also Richard Ellmann, "Wallace Stevens' Ice-Cream," *Kenyon Review*, xix (1957), pp. 89 ff., and Blackmur, "Examples of Wallace Stevens."

57. *C.P.*, pp. 79, 97, 50, 49.

58. Taupin, *L'Influence du Symbolisme Français*, p. 278.

59. See especially Winters, "Wallace Stevens," and Blackmur, "Examples of Wallace Stevens."

60. *O.P.*, p. 158.

61. cf. *N.S.F.*, i. i, *C.P.*, p. 380.

62. The stanzas entitled "The Naked Eye of My Aunt," which Morse calls "Stanzas for 'Le Monocle de Mon Oncle'," are, I think, self-parody of a joking kind, and can never have been intended for the poem (*O.P.*, p. 19).

63. Prologue to *N.S.F.*, *C.P.*, p. 380.

64. "Examples of Wallace Stevens," p. 192.

65. There are entirely different interpretations, e.g. Pack, *Wallace Stevens*, pp. 9 ff.

66. Winters, "Wallace Stevens," p. 440.

67. cf. *N.S.F.*, iii. vii, *C.P.*, p. 403.

68. Winters, "Wallace Stevens," p. 458.

69. Louis L. Martz comments: "Winters has made a brilliant diagnosis of the malady; but he underestimates the patient's will to live." ("Wallace Stevens: The World as Meditation," *Yale Review*, xlvii [1958], pp. 517–36.)

70. Randall Jarrell, "Reflections on Wallace Stevens," in *Poetry and the Age* (1955), pp. 124–36.

71. "A Thought Revealed," ii, *C.P.*, p. 185.

72. *Adagia*, *O.P.*, p. 160.

73. H. W. Garrod, *Wordsworth* (1923), p. 26.

74. *The Complex Fate*, p. 171.

75. R. H. Pearce, "Wallace Stevens: The Life of the Imagination," *Publications of the Modern Language Association of America*, lxvi (1951), pp. 561–82.

76. Jacket-note to *Ideas of Order*; Pearce, "Wallace Stevens: The Life of the Imagination," p. 567.

77. *C.P.*, pp. 122–7.

78. "Like Decorations in a Nigger Cemetery," *C.P.*, p. 158.

79. Martz, "Wallace Stevens: The World as Meditation," p. 520.

80. *O.P.*, p. 210.

81. "Botanist on Alp (No. 2)," *C.P.*, p. 136.

82. Martz, "Wallace Stevens: The World as Meditation," p. 522.

83. "Sad Strains of a Gay Waltz," *C.P.*, p. 122. See the lecture "Imagination as Value," *N.A.*, pp. 131 ff.

CHAPTER III

OWL'S CLOVER, THE MAN WITH THE BLUE GUITAR, AND *PARTS OF A WORLD*

Out of an aesthetic that denies, in its extreme formulations, the very possibility of long poems, there emerged, in the long, paradoxical and difficult course of things, the major poems of the twentieth century. Stevens came independently to feel that he must give "prolonged attention to a single subject" even before the publication of *Harmonium*; he wanted to "do long stretches at a time," and "to be as obscure as possible until I have perfected an authentic and fluent speech for myself."[1] In the end it happened that the kind of long poem suited to his gift was the set of closely related meditations on a single theme, as in *Notes toward a Supreme Fiction*; his thoughts tended to collect in pools, not to surge forward, as he had tried to make them in "The Comedian as the Letter C." Within that form his peculiar fabulatory powers could combine with a final authenticity of meditation; but although *The Man with the Blue Guitar* (1937) is written in brief sections of ten to fourteen lines, it took Stevens nearly twenty years to arrive at the full maturity of the form in *Notes* (1942). Meanwhile he went on writing "a multitude of short poems." The expression is Coleridge's; he thought Wordsworth was damaging himself as a philosophical poet by devoting his time to them, and it may be that Stevens also wrote too many such. He was already working on *Owl's Clover* when *Ideas of Order* came out; and between then and *Notes* he wrote not only the sixty-three poems of *Parts of a World* (1942) but the considerable group of inferior short poems that appear between pp. 35 and 86 of *Opus Posthumous*.

Owl's Clover[2] came out piecemeal. The first section, "The Old Woman and the Statue," appeared in *The Southern Review* (Summer 1935). In that year Stanley Burnshaw, a Marxist critic, reviewed *Ideas of Order* in *The New Masses*, and criticised Stevens' apparent indifference to what was going on in the world, calling him "a man who, having lost his footing, now scrambles to stand up and keep his balance."[3] As it happened, this hostile notice touched upon a theme that was interesting Stevens (though very much in his own way, which was not, of course, Mr Burnshaw's) at the time. Speaking of "The Old Woman and the Statue" in 1937, he said:

> The subject I had in mind was the effect of the depression on the interest in art. I wanted a confronting of the world as it had been imagined in art and as it was then in fact. If I dropped into a gallery I found that I had no interest in what I saw. The air was charged with anxieties and tensions. . . . I wanted to deal with exactly such a subject and I chose that as a bit of reality, actuality, the contemporaneous. But I wanted the result to be poetry so far as I was able to write poetry. To be specific, I wanted to apply my own sensibility to something perfectly matter-of-fact. The result would be a disclosure of my own sensibility or individuality . . . certainly to myself. . . . The old woman is a symbol of those who suffered during the depression and the statue is a symbol of art, although in several poems of which *Owl's Clover* . . . consists, the statue is a variable symbol. While there is nothing automatic about the poem, nevertheless it has an automatic aspect in the sense that it is what I wanted it to be without knowing before it was written what I wanted it to be, even though I knew before it was written what I wanted to do.[4]

Political and economic reality interested Stevens as a poet precisely because, like reality in other aspects, it exerted a pressure—at this time an incapacitating pressure—on his imagination. As such it became an urgent subject for poetry, which is useless if it does not adhere to what is real, and grip the "essential prose." Hence the confrontation of old woman and statue—that statue which, henceforth, will recur in its variable capacity in Stevens' verse and prose. Hence also the exploratory mode of writing; this was always his way, and the last sentence quoted above usefully expresses a paradox familiar to all artists, but it is most marked in *Owl's Clover*, the parts of which have a special kind of fortuity. Stung perhaps by Mr Burnshaw, sure at any rate that Mr Burnshaw's was in the end an inferior approach to reality, Stevens called the second part of the poem "Mr. Burnshaw and the Statue," and published it separately. The remaining three sections appeared first in the Alcestis Press edition of 1936. Mr Burnshaw dropped out of the poem; his section was shortened and called "The Statue at the World's End"; and Stevens made many other revisions for the version given in *The Man with the Blue Guitar and Other Poems* (Knopf, 1937). But later he repudiated its "rhetoric" and omitted it from *Collected Poems*. The version in *Opus Posthumous* is the original one.

W. Van O'Connor seems to be alone in thinking *Owl's Clover* Stevens' "finest long poem."[5] It is certainly of interest in its relation to what came later; but it is, in itself, an almost total failure. One sees what Stevens meant by using the term "rhetoric" pejoratively here; there is much random noise, the dry clatter of uninterestingly queer diction and stiff rhythms. But it begins well. The statue in the park makes its proper effect:

> So much the sculptor had foreseen: autumn,
> The sky above the plaza widening
> Before the horses, clouds of bronze imposed
> On clouds of gold, and green engulfing bronze,
> The marble leaping in the storms of light.

What he had not foreseen was the old woman, "the bitter mind | In a flapping cloak." None of all this could "touch her eye":

> She was that tortured one,
> So destitute that nothing but herself
> Remained, and nothing of herself except
> A fear. . . .

This woman is Poverty, in the wide sense Stevens gives to the word; the suffering of the unemployed is only an aspect of it. This poverty is the victory of reality over the imagination; or, the failure of the *fonction fabulatrice*. It is a failure of art, in face of new and terrible pressures, to provide what the gods and myths and statues of the past did provide:

> a single shawl,
> Wrapped tightly round us, since we are poor, a warmth,
> A light, a power, the miraculous influence.[6]

The woman's poverty deprives the statue of form and nobility: "The mass of stone collapsed to marble hulk," the very light "falls falsely" on it. Under the woman's influence, the formlessness of night becomes the "sovereign shape."

Against this the imagination contends in different ways. One is the poet's: "the great poems of heaven and hell have been written and the great poem of earth remains to be written"; and this is his objective. Another is the Communist's, Mr Burnshaw's; "with the collapse of other beliefs, this grubby faith promises a practicable earthly paradise." The values of the poet and of Mr Burnshaw are incompatible, but are alike the work of the imagination, and both seek "the normal in the abnormal, the opposite of chaos in chaos."[7] But Mr Burnshaw rejects the statue:

> The thing is dead. . . . Everything is dead
> Except the future. . . .
> These are not even Russian animals.

The dead heroic will go and be replaced by a heap of stones which "shall be carved, '*The Mass | Appoints These Marbles of Itself To Be | Itself.*' " The poet, on the other hand, rejects Mr Burnshaw and his "hopeful waste to come," his "age of concentric mobs." But what he offers instead is made much clearer in "Imagination as Value" than in *Owl's Clover*, and so is the contrast, upon which much of the poem dwells, between the poet's self-scrutiny and care for the real on the one hand and what he calls Africa, the modern world "of dense, savage, mindless animality" on the other.[8] The lecture speaks of "the universal mind, which, in the case of the poet, would be the imagination that tries to penetrate to basic images, basic emotions, and so to compose a fundamental poetry even older than the ancient world."[9] The poem supposes, in its final section, a subman, "The man below the man below the man":

> We have grown weary of the man that thinks.
> He thinks and it is not true. The man below
> Imagines and it is true. . . .

This old Adam "dwells below . . . in less | Than body and in less than mind, ogre." It seems he will be the defence against the rational State; that he will come to terms with the night instead of with the obsolete statue.

A few poems in *Parts of a World* echo this solution; it is interesting that Stevens' direct allusions to the intellectual Communism of the Thirties go no farther, but that the symbolism of the noble statue (and that of the night) grow into the fabric of his later work.

The Man with the Blue Guitar (1937)[10] is an advance toward the mature form of Stevens' long poems, and in itself a notable and original achievement. Also it is true

that an understanding of it brings the reward of familiarity
with many of the ideas and images of the later poetry.
It represents, in its taut couplets and gnomic diction, a
healthy constriction after *Owl's Clover*. "The opium-
drugged subman" is "erased, along with the style in
which he had been expressed. In his place we will have
something like Picasso's clear, clean image of the old
Guitar Player."[11] No more "rhetoric": instead, thirty-
three pools of astringent thought on imagination and
reality, on "the incessant conjunctioning between things
as they are and things imagined."[12] There is to be no
falsification. "In poetry at least the imagination must
not detach itself from reality."[13] Here are more adages
that help to explain *The Man with the Blue Guitar*:

The final poem ... will be the poem of fact not
realized before.

Perhaps there is a degree of perception at which what
is real and what is imagined are one: a state of clair-
voyant observation, accessible or possibly accessible to
the poet, or, say, the acutest poet.

The ultimate value is reality.

The great conquest is the conquest of reality.

It is not enough to present life, for a moment, as it
might have been.

The great poem is the disengaging of [a] reality.

The world is myself. Life is myself.

The poet is the intermediary between people and the
world in which they live and also, between people as
between themselves; but not between people and some
other world.[14]

The first poem equips the paradox (the imagination
must transform reality without changing it) with a set of
symbols:

The man bent over his guitar,
A shearsman of sorts. The day was green.

They said, "You have a blue guitar,
You do not play things as they are."

The man replied, "Things as they are
Are changed upon the blue guitar."

And they said then, "But play, you must,
A tune beyond us, yet ourselves,

A tune upon the blue guitar
Of things exactly as they are."

A shearsman, presumably because of the family of bar-
bers, who "lived in vain" because "not one curl in
nature has survived."[15] Something is wrong with his
playing; the problem is that the guitar (imagination) is
blue, and reality is green (this colour-system, with varia-
tions, persists throughout Stevens' poetry), and that the
guitar must, to be useful, abstain from falsifying reality
("the ultimate value"). Order-in-chaos is a creation of
the human mind; therefore the song must be "ourselves";
but since something is added (imagination) to that reality
which is "ourselves," the tune must also be "beyond us."
The second section admits the guitarist's failure quite to
achieve this: "I sing a hero's head, large eye | And
bearded bronze, but not a man." (This "hero," creator
of things as they ultimately are, with the light of imagination upon them, is to be almost ubiquitous in the sub-
sequent poetry.) Sect. iii concerns the difficulty of appre-
hending the real quality of the human mind; sect. iv, the
difficult multiplicity of men. The multitude of men
speak in sect. v; the old poetry is dead, "The earth, for
us, is flat and bare." "Ourselves" need a poetry that will
"take the place | Of empty heaven and its hymns," a
poetry in which they have a place. Sect. vi enlarges this;
the tune must produce one of those moments of balance

between the human mind and its environment, moments in which "The thinking of art seems final when | The thinking of god is smoky dew." In Sect. vii, the sun is, as always, the fountain of reality, the moon of imagination. The blue of the guitar can hardly be seen against the final blue of the sky, which is, as the limit of his perception, the last word on the poet's "things as they are." ("Weather," in Sect. ix, is another idea which, as affecting the relation of imagination to the world, occurs in, for example, *Notes toward a Supreme Fiction*.)

Sects. x and xi deal with the failure of imagination (Sect. xi is very fine, and a new effect in Stevens). Sect. xii isolates the hero-poet, creator of reality;[16] Sect. xiii deals obscurely with "gaudy" errors of imagination, which detract from the real blue. Sect. xiv beautifully uses the image of the candle (the light of imagination),[17] and Sect. xv alludes again to the *Owl's Clover* theme of the failure of imagination to connect and enrich. Sect. xvi develops this in a different figure; we are no longer children of the earth. Sect. xvii emphasises this new animalism, which makes the guitar a hollow and worthless instrument. But in Sect. xviii the reality of its tune is asserted; it produces not a dream, but a thing of things as they are, made real, as by light falling on them. Sect. xix is a prayer, that the poet should contain and master, rather than be, the human monster. But (sect. xx) ideas are not things; to believe is the desirable, the missing power. Sect. xxi reverts to the "hero," here as later associated with the mountain Chocorua.[18] He must take the place of God, a shadow of man but "without shadows, without magnificence." We move closer to the central hero of Stevens' later poetry; "the major abstraction is the idea of man."[19]

Poetry (the whole power of the imagination) is the subject of all poems; in covering it they make contact with reality, adding to as well as taking from it (sect. xxii). This is the dependence upon one another of "things

of opposite natures,"[20] "thought | And the truth,
Dichtung und Wahrheit." Their union in a phrase, a
page, or a book, is joy, like the scholar's joy[21] (sect. xxiv).
"Poetry," says Stevens, "is the scholar's art."[22] Sect. xxv
is a comic account of the world controlled by the poet;
sects. xxvi and xxvii speak of the opposition to his
"murderous alphabet," especially from the sea, again
the basic, inarticulate reality. Sect. xxviii has a familiar
theme; he lives in the world, not in his mind, and thinks
"like a native"—"as I am, I speak and move | And things
are as I think they are." Sect. xxix celebrates that resemblance which is never identity, and which makes art
possible.[23] Sect. xxx is the first picture of "major man,"[24]
seen against an obscure subtopian background. Sect.
xxxi is another view of the peculiar hostility of modern
life to the imagination. In sect. xxxii the need of absolute
novelty in the pursuit of things as they are—one as one
is—is the topic; and finally (sect. xxxiii) we return to the
scene familiar from *Owl's Clover*: the stony reality of now,
the bread promised in a future State, and a neglect of
reality, except when the imagination recovers it.

The Blue Guitar is a difficult poem, and these notes are
starting-places for argument and rebuttal, no more.
Much of the verse—"the crisp common diction, the
strict driving rhythm of the short couplets, subtly bound
together by irregular rhymes and half-rhymes"[25]—is
admirable and new. What it lacks is the emotional progression that is a feature of *Notes toward a Supreme Fiction*,
the rich illusion that the poem itself is moving toward a
revelation, however obscure that end and the means to
it. But it takes us a long way up-country from *Harmonium*.

Of the other poems published with *The Blue Guitar*, "A
Thought Revolved" (*C.P.*, p. 184) should be mentioned.
Its first section was singled out by Winters for special
condemnation.[26] The second, "Mystic Garden and Middling Beast," has exceptional doctrinal importance. The
poet, deeply concerned with the abstract,[27] is deeply

involved in "the idea of man," man considered as the fiction-maker, the giver of order. This man is the heart of poetry in our time, the subject of the poet's hymns, "Happy rather than holy," because this is the joy that has to do the work of the old Heaven, and concerned with Earth as a paradise, but also with man in general as not an angel but merely "a middling beast." The notion is present in the third section also: the hero is "Son only of man and sun of men,"

> With all his attributes no god but man
> Of men whose heaven is in themselves,
>
> Or else whose hell. . . .

And, I think, the fourth introduces us to the "antimasterman,"[28] corrupted by intellect, who brings death to the universe of man: "his great toe like a horn, | The central flaw in the solar morn." (Horn is the deathcolour in Stevens.)

In that short sequence Stevens was revolving thoughts which came to be more fully fleshed later. Some are in *Parts of a World*, the collection of 1942. This book is nobody's favourite, though it contains many poems of very high quality. It is a book in which the poems do little to quicken each other, and the worst way to approach it is to try and read it through. Its main topic is the exteriority of things, but it is philosophically considered; the thought is revolved, not transmuted into those images which woke in the poet's blood for *Notes toward a Supreme Fiction*.

For one of the poems in this volume Stevens found his aptest epigraph: *Je tâche, en restant exact, d'être poète.*[29] This is the whole problem; to transform the world, bring summer into winter and riches into poverty, without altering it to take the parts of a world and make an order, or, as the opening poem puts it, "Piece the world to-

gether boys, but not with your hands."[30] Between the
world of fact and the desires of men there is a gulf,
beautifully defined in "The Poems of our Climate,"[31]
where we are given an object: "Clear water in a brilliant
bowl, | Pink and white carnations," which does not
suffice. "One desires | So much more than that." Even if
it were capable in itself of cleaning or redeeming us, it
would not suffice.

> There would still remain the never-resting mind . . .
> The imperfect is our paradise.
> Note that, in this bitterness, delight,
> Since the imperfect is so hot in us,
> Lies in flawed words and stubborn sounds.

Nothing will suffice but a poem, an act of imagination, a
rendering of the speechless object in human terms. "The
squirming facts exceed the squamous mind, | If one may
say so. And yet relation appears."[32] The relation is, of
course, the work of imagination, for "The reason can
give nothing at all | Like the response to desire." The
human senses cannot account for what the mind does to
reality, witness what it can do to a pineapple:

> the buxom eye merely brings its element
> To the total thing, a shapeless giant forced
> Upward.
>   Green were the curls upon that head.[33]

The mind is projected on to reality:

> The hand between the candle and the wall
> Grows large on the wall. . . .
>
> It must be that the hand
> Has a will to grow larger on the wall,
> To grow larger and heavier and stronger than

The wall; and that the mind
Turns to its own figurations and declares,
"*This image, this love, I compose myself*
Of these. In these, I come forth outwardly.
In these, I wear a vital cleanliness,
Not as in air, bright-blue-resembling air,
But as in the powerful mirror of my wish and will."[34]

This is the image of the world that suffices, and gives
solace, and the power to live in this world and its
"weather." There is (sect. vii) a splendid passage, too
long to quote, on this sufficing of the mind in "Extracts
from Addresses to the Academy of Fine Ideas." (*C.P.*, p.
257.) If the physical world may by this means satisfy the
mind, then "one's belief | Resists each past apocalypse"
—the falsifying explanations of myth and religion—and
"belief in one's element," or "Ecstatic identies | Between
one's self and the weather" suffice:

> it is enough
> To believe in the weather and in the things and men
> Of the weather and in one's self, as part of that
> And nothing more.

In any other world one could not believe, not make that
which suffices; but if one returned from such a world,
say the moon, to the earth, even if the earth were hardly
lit and almost devoid of colour, "naked of any illusion, in
poverty," one would at once breathe the sufficient air
and be at home.

The idea of the poem as the "act of finding | What will
suffice" occurs in "Man and Bottle" (*C.P.*, p. 238),
where the harshness and hostility of reality are related to
the war; and in "Of Modern Poetry,"[35] which opens with
the words just quoted. The mind which performs this
act is called "More than a man. . . . A man with the fury
of a race of men, A light at the centre of many lights, | A
man at the centre of men." And this, the human mind

which creates the fictions by which reality comes to
suffice, is Stevens' major man, his abstraction from
humanity, his central poet. The poet "creates the world
to which we turn incessantly and without knowing it
and . . . gives life to the supreme fictions without which
we are unable to conceive it."[36]

> Poet, patting more nonsense foamed
> From the sea, conceive for the courts
> Of these academies, the diviner health
> Disclosed in common forms. . . .
> We are conceived in your conceits.[37]

The man who can put together the parts of the world
and make what suffices is major man, the modern god.
He is really a way of speaking of the imagination in a
world where God no longer works. "Man must become
the hero of his world";[38] his union with reality is an act
of his mind. Thus the hero *is* all men, and lives in their
poverty, as he himself says in "Idiom of the Hero": (*C.P.*,
p. 201) "I am the poorest of all."

The examination of this hero is one of the major pre-
occupations of the volume; and this makes it, among
other things, indispensable as a prelude to *Notes toward a
Supreme Fiction*. The most direct treatment of the image
occurs in "Asides on the Oboe" (*C.P.*, p. 250), and
"Examination of the Hero in a Time of War" (*C.P.*, p.
273).

The first of these is a remarkably complete handling
of the metaphysical positions considered in *Parts of a
World*. Belief, as we learnt from "The Academy of Fine
Ideas," must finally be in this world, but in this world
as the imagination conceives it: and this is the great
Fiction. The old fictions—myth, religion, the noble hero
whose statue is now crumbling[39]—are obsolete; but the
mind that makes the fictions survives, a Man abstracted
from the idea of man-in-his-world:

> The philosophers' man alone still walks in dew,
> Still by the sea-side mutters milky lines
> Concerning an immaculate imagery.

"By the sea-side," that is, ordering the sea with song. He is "the man who has had the time to think enough, | The central man"—

> He is the transparence of the place in which
> He is and in his poems we find peace.

He is "the glass man," who "dewily cries, 'Thou art not August unless I make thee so.' " Writing to Henry Church in 1940 about a scheme for a Chair of Poetry at Princeton, Stevens said: "The subject-matter of poetry is the thing to be ascertained. Offhand, the subject-matter is what comes to mind when one says of the month of August . . . "Thou are not August, unless I make thee so."[40] August is the season of the mind's satisfaction, when the earth suffices; but this sufficiency is the work of the hero. So is all the order and wholeness of earth, including evil and death: "We found, | If we found the central evil, the central good." "Asides on the Oboe," though a fine poem in itself, is a rehearsal for *Notes toward a Supreme Fiction* and "Esthétique du Mal."

"Examination of the Hero" affirms the hero's "commonness," but also the icy winter reality he reconciles with the satisfactions of August:

> make him of winter's
> Iciest core, a north star, central
> In our oblivion, of summer's
> Imagination, the golden rescue.

He is a primitive figure because the emotions are archaic; but still "we have and are the man." He "acts in reality, adds nothing | To what he does." He is "the highest man with nothing higher | Than himself."

Opposed to this hero is the "anti-master-man," who

rejects all the fictions, the alive as well as the dead,
"Nabob | Of bones," who "never supposed" ("Landscape
with Boat," *C.P.*, p. 241):

> That he might be truth, himself, or part of it,
> That the things he rejected might be part
> And the irregular turquoise, part, the perceptible blue
> Grown denser, part, the eye so touched, so played
> Upon by clouds, the ear so magnified
> By thunder, parts, and all these things together,
> Parts, and more things, parts. He never supposed divine
> Things might not look divine, nor that if nothing
> Was divine then all things were, the world itself,
> And that if nothing was the truth, then all
> Things were the truth, the world itself was the truth.

The true hero, then, is the human fictive power applied
to reality. I have dwelt on the development of this idea in
Parts of a World because it is the theme of many rich
repetitions later; and so are some associated ideas. That
of change, made necessary to the fiction by alteration of
the mutual stance of reality and the hero (the subject of
the first part of *Notes*) is treated fully in "The Man on the
Dump" (*C.P.*, p. 201). That of the fortuity of poetic discovery, another theme of *Notes*, occurs in "The Sense of
the Sleight-of-Hand Man" (*C.P.*, p. 222). The special
sense of "weather," mentioned above and also important
in *Notes*, is found again in the fine "Martial Cadenza"
(*C.P.*, p. 237). And one of the best poems in the volume,
"A Rabbit as King of the Ghosts" (*C.P.*, p. 209), is a
handling of another theme in *Notes*, the animal consciousness imposing its order on reality, as opposed (here
tacitly) to the human, which discovers an order without
imposing it.

Parts of a World is more various than I have allowed it to
appear. It even has a poem that is, although serious,
funny: "Loneliness in Jersey City" (*C.P.*, p. 210). But it
is preoccupied with that knowledge of the harshness and

poverty of reality which was present but did not openly declare itself in *Harmonium*; Stevens specifically alludes to the difference in "Montrachet-le-Jardin" (*C.P.*, p. 263):

> A little while of Terra Paradise
> I dreamed, of autumn rivers, silvas green,
> Of sanctimonious mountains high in snow,
>
> But in that dream a heavy difference
> Kept waking and a mournful sense sought out,
> In vain, life's season or death's element.

The study of this heavy difference brings Stevens not to a sophisticated acceptance of one of the dead myths, as it brought Yeats, Eliot, and Pound, but to the creation of this new myth of the hero. At the end of the long and relatively dry period treated in this chapter, Stevens had prepared, in "practice poems," an imagery which might be equal, at last, to all the demands of the long poem he wanted to write. And indeed this poem, *Notes toward a Supreme Fiction*, was first published in 1942, the same year as *Parts of a World*.

REFERENCES

1. Letter to Harriet Monroe; Morse, Preface to *O.P.*, pp. xxi–xxii.
2. *O.P.*, pp. 43–71.
3. Martz, "Wallace Stevens: The World as Meditation," p. 524.
4. "The Irrational Element in Poetry," *O.P.*, pp. 219–220.
5. *Shaping Spirit*, p. 60.
6. "Final Soliloquy of the Interior Paramour," *C.P.*, p. 524.
7. Prose quotations in this paragraph all come from "Imagination as Value," *N.A.*, pp. 133–56.
8. Martz, "Wallace Stevens: The World as Meditation," p. 525.
9. "I.V.," *N.A.*, p. 145.

10. *C.P.*, pp. 165–84. There are interesting rejected stanzas in *O.P.*, pp. 72–3.

11. Martz, "Wallace Stevens: The World as Meditation," p. 526. He adds that the painting (in which the guitar is coloured tan) was exhibited in Hartford in 1934.

12. Jacket-note by Stevens, quoted by Pearce, "Wallace Stevens: The Life of the Imagination," p. 569.

13. *Adagia*, *O.P.*, p. 161.

14. *O.P.*, pp. 164, 166, 168, 169, 173, 172, 162.

15. But see Pearce, "Wallace Stevens: The Life of the Imagination," p. 569.

16. See below, pp. 74 ff.

17. See above, p. 7.

18. See "Chocorua to its Neighbor," *C.P.*, pp. 296 ff., and below, p. 101 f.
    The mountain in Vermont is called Chocoru; for legendary associations see O'Connor, *Shaping Spirit*, p. 81.

19. *N.S.F.*, I. x, *C.P.*, p. 388.

20. *N.S.F.*, II. iv, *C.P.*, p. 392.

21. *N.S.F.*, II. vii, *C.P.*, p. 395.

22. *Adagia*, *O.P.*, p. 167.

23. See below, p. 89.

24. cf. *N.S.F.*, I. x, *C.P.*, pp. 388–9.

25. Martz, "Wallace Stevens: The World as Meditation," p. 527.

26. "Wallace Stevens, or, the Hedonist's Progress," pp. 445–6.

27. See p. 51 above, and pp. 112 ff. below.

28. "Landscape with Boat," *C.P.*, pp. 241 ff.; and see below, pp. 75–6.

29. Jules Renard; "United Dames of America," *C.P.*, p. 206.

30. "Parochial Theme," *C.P.*, p. 192.

31. *C.P.*, pp. 193–4. See also "Study of Two Pears," (*C.P.*, p. 196) on the theme "The plum survives its poems." And cf. "Bouquet of Roses in Sunlight," *C.P.*, p. 430.

32. "Connoisseur of Chaos," *C.P.*, p. 215.

33. "Poem Written at Morning," *C.P.*, p. 219. Cf. "Someone puts a Pineapple together," *N.A.* pp. 83 ff.

34. "Poem with Rhythms," *C.P.*, pp. 245–6.

35. *C.P.*, pp. 239–40. See also "The Well Dressed Man with the Beard," *C.P.*, p. 247.

36. "The Noble Rider and the Sound of Words," *N.A.*, p. 31.

37. "Prelude to Objects," *C.P.*, p. 195.

38. "Montrachet-le-Jardin," *C.P.*, p. 261.

39. Cf. *Owl's Clover* and *N.R.*; and *N.S.F.*, II. iii, *C.P.*, p. 391.

40. Morse, Preface to *O.P.*, p. xiv.

CHAPTER IV

PROSE WORKS

In so short a study of a difficult poet it has seemed reason-
able to devote most of the space to the verse; but it is out
of the question to omit the prose of Stevens altogether,
because it illuminates the poetry, is in itself a kind of
poetry, and seems at present, to judge by the chilly and
uncomprehending reception given by English reviewers
to *The Necessary Angel*, in some need of apology. It is dealt
with here because the greater part of it was written between 1942 and 1951, and because it is a useful preliminary to the long poems of the forties. This interlude
also provides an opportunity to say the briefest of words
on Stevens' philosophical sources.

I have already drawn on the *Adagia*,[1] might have used
them even more, and would like to study them at length
in this chapter; but this is impossible, and it is, anyway,
enough to say that they are vital to any understanding of
Stevens, and that, as a collection of *obiter dicta* on poetry
by a working poet, they are probably unmatched since
Hopkins. They turn up regularly not only in the prose
but in the poems, sometimes unchanged, sometimes
transformed. Thus "Poetry is the gaiety (joy) of language"[2] is the basis of the unforgettable couplet:

> Natives of poverty, children of malheur,
> The gaiety of language is our seigneur.[3]

"The poem reveals itself only to the ignorant man,"[4] a
conventional enough doctrine for a modern poet to hold,
is expanded in *Notes toward a Supreme Fiction*, I. i; "To be at
the end of fact is not to be at the beginning of imagina-

tion, but it is to be at the end of both,"[5] is, as we have
seen, a doctrine that Stevens meditated deeply, but in
Notes (III. vi) Stevens remembered this formula in the
middle of one of his most extended and superb flights.
On the other hand, "God and the imagination are one,"
and "The death of one god is the death of all" go without
alteration into poems.[6] The *Adagia* are not all equally
interesting, of course, and they are a little repetitious,
but they are a remarkable assembly of work-notes which
have often their own intrinsic value as topics for meditation. They are *sui generis*, though in manner there is
sometimes a slight resemblance to the aphorisms of
Emerson.

Other notebooks, incidentally, survive, and Morse
says they demonstrate wide reading.[7] This would be
obvious anyway; a single lecture contains allusions, more
or less in passing, to statements of F. W. Bateson,
Bergson, Busoni, Coleridge, Croce, Freud, Rostrevor
Hamilton, Joad, Pareto, I. A. Richards, Robert Wolseley,
and Virginia Woolf.[8] These are mostly chance illustrations. It would be absurd to labour the point, had there not
been lately some suggestion that Stevens did his reading
and thinking at second hand; this notion is fostered by
the candour with which he says "Jean Wahl wrote to me,
saying . . ." or "Jean Paulhan sent me some notes"—or
quotes Joad on logical positivism, or admits to using a
student's history of philosophy.[9] These sources were perfectly adequate to his purposes; he never claimed to
think as a philosopher. "The probing of the philosopher
is deliberate as the probing of the poet is fortuitous."[10]
Indeed he regarded philosophy, the differences of which
from poetry he often tried to define,[11] as part of his *materia
poetica*. This seems to have been his way of reading everything.

He does, however, confess a specific debt to Focillon,[12]
obviously owes much to Mallarmé and to Valéry,[13] and
above all to Santayana and Bergson, whom he presum-

ably absorbed in his youth. *Interpretations of Poetry and Religion* (1900) is a key book for the thought of Stevens: here are three extracts which suggest how direct the influence must have been: the poet

> disintegrates the fictions of common perception into their sensuous elements, gathers these together again into chance groups, as the accidents of his environment or the affinities of his temperament may conjoin them; and this wealth of sensation and this freedom of fancy, which make an extraordinary ferment in his ignorant heart, presently bubble over into some kind of utterance (p. 260).

> The great function of poetry . . . is . . . to repair to the material of experience, seizing hold of the reality of sensation and fancy beneath the surface of conventional ideas, and then out of that living but indefinite material to build new structures, richer, finer, fitted to the primary tendencies of our nature. . . (p. 270).

The last words of the book speak of

> the sphere of significant imagination, of relevant fiction, of idealism become the interpretation of the reality it leaves behind. Poetry raised to its highest power is then identical with religion grasped in its inmost truth; at their point of union both reach their utmost purity and beneficence, for then poetry loses its frivolity and ceases to demoralize, while religion surrenders its illusions and ceases to deceive (p. 290).

Again, in *Reason and Art*, Santayana says that the "rational poet's vision would have the same moral functions that myth was asked to fulfil, and fulfilled so treacherously; it would employ the same ideal faculties which myth used confusedly" (p. 224). It would be easy to multiply such passages. Stevens would not always have accepted every nuance of those I have quoted; but they contain a proportion of his own thought hardly explicable except in terms of direct influence. The general injunction, "It must give pleasure," is good Santayana. He admired Santayana's early poetry, and above all the philosopher's life, of which he wrote movingly both in "Imagination as Value",[14] and in a great poem of his old age, "To an Old Philosopher in Rome."[15]

The debt to Bergson is quite certain, though nowhere explicitly acknowledged even where Bergson is quoted. I have spoken above of the similarity between Stevens' doctrine of the saving imagination and the Bergsonian *fonction fabulatrice*;[16] this biologically essential function can, for Stevens, be performed only by poetry, and not, as Bergson thought, by metaphysics. But the new poetry must be related to modern reality, and so "it must change." Poets invented gods and myths, they invented Heaven and Hell; but all these are irrelevant to modern reality,

> since now both heaven and hell
> Are one and here, O terra infidel.[17]

The necessary poem is now of the earth; this is a theme meditated repeatedly in the essays, and endlessly in poems which seek to be true not only to the defensive fiction but to the chaos gleaming behind it; to fortuity and freshness as well as to order. The union of imagination and reality is constantly shifting, constantly in need of renewal; and nowhere, so far as I know, is Stevens' thought on this subject more closely anticipated than in Bergson's *Le temps et le mouvant*, where the shifting relation of subject and object also leads to the conclusion, equally congenial to Stevens, that reality is irreducible to conventional philosophical concepts. Stevens' "revelations of reality"[18] are things seen, as Bergson puts it, *sub specie durationis*. Stevens might have had this from other sources; but as it seems so likely that he read

Bergson attentively, we may well think Bergson the source.

Stevens also read later philosophy, but without much doubt he was most affected by these older writers. Bergson and Santayana provide strong philosophical links with the Romantic-Symbolist tradition in which Stevens as a poet inevitably found himself, and they provided him with ways of thinking about the world as transformed by the mind. The poems, though philosophical, are never philosophy; they aspire to that condition of philosophical poetry which Coleridge thought to be within the power of Wordsworth, whose theme was also the interdependence of imagination and reality. Such poetry differs from philosophy in that it is "part of the *res* itself and not about it."[19] The poem is not a comment but a fact never before realised, a contribution to reality. Compared with philosophy it is disorderly, because it depends on *trouvailles*,[20] and because it has an indispensable element of unreason. The *fonction fabulatrice* is irrational; so is metaphor (resemblance pleases in so far as it is not identity). Finally, the reality of poetry is a reality "flicked by feeling."[21] "The irrational element in poetry is the transaction between reality and the sensibility of the poet from which poetry springs."[22]

Stevens' lectures and essays are prose-poems of a very curious kind. They are in some ways like the late discourses of Valéry; a little ingrown, a little repetitive, strangely blending the workaday diction of the lecturer with the more habitual splendour of the poet. He came late to lecturing, and his thinking in prose is conditioned by years of thinking in poetry. In poetry, he said, one discloses poetry; in prose one tries to disclose definitions of poetry.[23] But he arrived at these definitions by strange routes. If he was a metaphysician he was so—as Coleridge said poets ought to be—*implicitè*, not *explicitè*. The essays are constructed like meditative poems, circling beautifully around central images, proceeding with a grave gaiety to repetitive but ever-changing statements about the imagination, "the one reality in this imagined world," and about the poet who seeks "what will suffice" to refresh an earth to which God is no longer relevant. The imagination creates evil as well as good, political and all other values; but as poetry it is the sun of the mind, bringer of savour and health, destroyer of poverty.

Stevens sometimes thought of the poet (and the poem) as a kind of hermit, going and coming into life and language,[24] and these are the hermit's public appearances; respecting the conventions in his unfamiliar grey suit of academic prose, yet unchanged, vivid, committed to his own speech. The lectures give a new dimension to Stevens; his claims for poetry are vast, and this dash of academic sobriety helps one to understand that they are not merely fine talk. The poet speaks the "words of the world" that "are the life of the world."[25] How vast this and kindred claims really are can be seen if one thinks, for instance, of Mr Eliot, who believes that art has frontiers, and that one goes on from it to other and possibly more important matters. Stevens' poet discovers an order which cannot be discovered by anybody else; religion, myth, were forms of poetic activity—"poetry intervening in life," as Santayana put it—but now finally out of touch with reality. The full modern reality is "a reality of decreation," said Stevens, borrowing an expression of Simone Weil, "in which our revelations are not the revelations of belief, but the precious portents of our own powers."[26]

> The freshness of transformation is
> The freshness of a world. It is our own,
> It is ourselves, the freshness of ourselves.[27]

The poet who effects this transformation, this "conversion of our *Lumpenwelt*"[28] has invoked "the necessary angel" in whose sight we

see the earth again,
Cleared of its stiff and stubborn, man-locked set.[29]

The Necessary Angel: Essays on Reality and the Imagination
(1951, 1960) is a collection of lectures given between 1942
and 1951. It is worth explaining how it came by its title.
In 1949 Stevens bought a still-life by Tal Coat; he admired it because "for all its in-door light on in-door
objects, the picture refreshes us with an out-door sense of
things." (He is writing to his bookseller in Paris; but
already the language of the letter is half-remembering
the imagery of weather, and the imagination is an
"in-door light.") He conferred upon this picture the
fanciful title, "Angel surrounded by Peasants," the angel
being "the Venetian glass bowl on the left," and the
peasants the objects surrounding it. Then he described it,
in language exactly appropriate to his own poems, as an
"effort to attain a certain reality purely by way of the
artist's own vitality." The next stage was the poem "Angel
surrounded by Paysans," which Stevens placed at the
end of *Auroras of Autumn* (1950). The angel which grew
out of the Venetian glass there becomes the imagination
which redeems the earth; he tells the peasants that he has
"neither ashen wing nor wear of ore," and that he is one
of them, yet "the necessary angel of the earth." In the
following year, after much deliberation, he consented to
the publication of a collection of lectures and essays, and
the angel out of the Venetian glass furnished its title.
This seems characteristic of the interaction of idea and
image in Stevens; a work of art promoted meditation;
meditation produces images, capable of endless variation.
The angel had made an independent appearance in the
same role in the greatest of all Stevens' poetry, *Notes
toward a Supreme Fiction*, III. vi–viii.[30]

The first chapter of *The Necessary Angel* is almost contemporaneous with *Notes*, and the connexion between
the two works is close. "The Noble Rider and the Sound

of Words" is almost the first, and one of the most impressive, of the attempts to present poetry as "one of the enlargements of life."[31] It is arranged as a commentary on a series of images of noble riders: the charioteer of the *Phaedrus*, Don Quixote, Verrocchio's equestrian statue of Colleone, a statue of General Jackson in Washington, and a painting by a modern American artist of a merry-go-round. (Stevens returns here to the statue symbol of *Owl's Clover* and elsewhere, notably the statue of "General Du Puy" in *Notes*, ii. iii.) The charioteer of Plato is obsolete, "the emblem of a mythology, the rustic memorial of a belief in the soul," because it no longer related to reality: "the imagination loses vitality as it ceases to adhere to what is real . . . the figure is all imagination. . . . We do not realise it." Similarly, Verrocchio's statue has a nobility which is false to reality: "the apposition between the imagination and the reality is too favourable to the imagination." This is because of a change in the relation between imagination and reality. The statue of Jackson is unreal because not a work of imagination; the merry-go-round picture, being "wholly favorable to what is real," is "not without imagination."

The failure, for us, of Plato and Verrocchio, is due to a change in the power of reality, which now presses harder upon the imagination. Stevens agrees with Freud (*The Future of an Illusion*) that we must come to terms with "the cruelty of reality," and cast off the "religious illusion"— but he differs in thinking that this is a matter not of intellectual but of imaginative effort. The pressure of modern reality Stevens defines as "the pressure of an external event or events on the consciousness to the exclusion of any power of contemplation." He writes of this in a time of war; but "the war is only a part of a war-like whole." At such a time the pressure is great enough to "bring about the end of one era in the history of the imagination" and to begin another; necessarily it is the determining factor of the art of an era. To provide the necessary imaginative resistance is the task of the poet.

This poet will have learned from the noble images of the past, but he knows modern reality, and knows that "his own measure as a poet . . . is the measure of his power to abstract himself, and to withdraw with him into his abstraction the reality on which the lovers of truth insist." He cannot be a very noble rider; he deals with things as they are. His poetry is "an interdependence of the imagination and reality as equals." He has no social or political obligation; such obligations are part of the pressure he must resist. "No politician can command the imagination. Stalin might grind his teeth the whole of a Russian winter and yet all the poets in the Soviets might remain silent the following spring." What, then, is his function?

Certainly it is not to lead people out of the confusion in which they find themselves. Nor is it, I think, to comfort them while they follow their leaders[32] to and fro. I think that his function is to make his imagination become the light in the minds of others. His role, in short, is to help people to live their lives.

He brings savour to life, dealing with it as the intellect cannot. If you want to use the word, Stevens allows you to call this escapism; but the sense of this word should be pejorative only when "the poet is not attached to reality." He saves the world out of poverty and "gives to life the supreme fictions without which we should be unable to conceive it." His words are literally the life of the world;[33] they "express our thoughts and feelings which, we are sure, are all the truth that we shall ever experience, having no illusions," and "we search the sound of them for a finality, a perfection, an unalterable vibration, which it is only within the power of the acutest poet to give them." They give life its nobility; they are the work of the mind that adds nothing to reality but resists it, preserving us and helping us to live our lives.

This strange and, I think, beautiful performance is a little marred by some thin passages on the history of ideas. The other chapters I must mention more briefly. "The Figure of the Youth as Virile Poet" (1943)[34] argues again for the poet's dependence on reality, his necessary dealings with reason, but insists on his need of "indirect egotism," because in his poetry he is always describing his own mind, and "he shares the transformation, not to say apotheosis, accomplished by the poem." This is something we all have, though in inferior degree;[35] but the poet's sense is communicable. His poem—especially his long poem—"comes to possess the reader and ... naturalizes him in its own imagination and liberates him there." "In this state of elevation," he goes on, introducing a paragraph of his most splendid prose, "we feel perfectly adapted to the idea that moves and *l'oiseau qui chante*."

If we say that the idea of God is merely a poetic idea, even if the supreme poetic idea, and that our notions of heaven and hell are merely poetry not so called, even if poetry that involves us vitally, the feeling of deliverance, of a release, of a perfection touched, of a vocation so that all men may know the truth and that the truth may set them free—if we say these things and if we are able to see the poet who achieved God and placed Him in His seat in heaven in all His glory, the poet himself, still in the ecstasy of the poem that completely accomplished his purpose, would have seemed, whether young or old, whether in rags or ceremonial robe, a man who needed what he had created, uttering the hymns of joy that followed his creation. This may be a gross exaggeration of a very simple matter. But perhaps that remark is true of many of the more prodigious things of life and death.

His "young" poet, the tamer of modern reality, bears
the lineaments of his noble ancestors; but he is concerned
with the truth only of credible things and his exaltation
comes of a "victory over the incredible." But he is apart
from the philosopher; for him *la vie est plus belle que les
idées*, and he lives in "a radiant and productive atmosphere" in which "the philosopher is an alien." "It is the
mundo of the imagination in which the imaginative man
delights and not the gaunt world of reason." He unites
reality with freshness and pleasure. But he brings in no
supernatural reality; the imagination, "like light, adds
nothing except itself." By means of a hymn to the Muse
that subtly changes as he repeats it, Stevens contrives to
end with a paradox; there is after all a "mystic muse," a
reality above the normal, as the truth of imagination is
above that of the falsifying intellect.

"The Figure of the Youth" is in many ways the most
perfectly achieved of these lectures, and has the usual
virtues of illustrating poems. "Three Academic Pieces"
(1947)[36] is a lesser though still an important work, and I
have already used it in commenting upon Stevens' doctrine that "poetry is a satisfying of the desire for resemblance."[37] Two brief passages may, however, be quoted:

What our eyes behold may well be the text of life but
one's meditations on the text and the disclosures of
these meditations are no less a part of the structure of
reality.

The brilliance of earth is the brilliance of every paradise.

The argument in "Effects of Analogy" (1948)[38] again
turns upon the poet as concerned with the operations by
which imagination uses reality; the poet's subject is "his
sense of the world," and this necessarily secludes him
from other men; if you want to call his cult of his own

personality by pejorative terms such as "ivory tower," you may; but this is how he has to go about his business of finding the words which make "a world that transcends the world and a life livable in that transcendence." These words, or poetry, constitute "a transcendent analogue composed of the particulars of reality, created by the poet's sense of the world."

"Imagination as Value" (1948)[39] is one of the most rewarding of the lectures. In it, Stevens considers the imagination as the delusive force it seemed to Pascal, who nevertheless returned to it for consolation in death, and goes on to cleanse his conception of the beneficent imagination from the charge that as a metaphysical term it means nothing; from the falsities entailed upon it by its Romantic associations; from the intellectualism of Freud, already discussed in "The Noble Rider." He considers the part of imagination in other approaches to reality than those of art, and of its varying aspect at different times and in different places. But there is a basic difference between the imagination that is satisfied by, say, politics, and that which "tries to penetrate to basic images, basic emotions," in order to "compose a fundamental poetry even older than the ancient world." The imagination penetrates life; but it is a different force in art, and a force essential to life. It "enables us to perceive the normal in the abnormal, the opposite of chaos in chaos." Its "instantaneous disclosures" are "disclosures of the normal." The lecture ends with a great passage in praise of imagination as the human defence against "poverty," and another use of the statue image. "The chief problems of any artist, as of any man, are the problems of the normal, and . . . he needs, in order to solve them, everything that the imagination has to give."

"Imagination as Value" is a difficult lecture, but many of its basic positions are hinted at in the earlier prose; and somewhere far behind it lies the Coleridgian distinction between primary and secondary imagination. The last essay in *The Necessary Angel*, "The Relations between Poetry and Painting,"[40] happens to be on another traditional topic. It compares the "plausibility and bigotry" of modern painting with that of modern poetry; but chiefly it asserts—with much illustration and discrimination—that "in an age in which disbelief is so profoundly prevalent or, if not disbelief, indifference to questions of belief, poetry and painting . . . are . . . a compensation for what has been lost." The imagination operating in this work "is to be regarded not as a phase of humanism but as a vital self-assertion in a world in which nothing but the self remains, if that remains." The interest of this essay is that Stevens here considers the work of his contemporaries in relation to the huge burdens he places upon the arts as "sources of our present conception of reality."

Of the prose printed in *Opus Posthumous* the earliest is "The Irrational Element in Poetry" (1937?),[41] which seems to say that this irrationality, with the modern sanction of Freud, of Mallarmé and Rimbaud, is an essential part of the poetic force that resists "the pressure of the contemporaneous." It shows in the irrationally chosen subject of art: "The only possible resistance . . . is a matter of herrings and apples." The poet is always looking for something new, suddenly come upon, a metamorphosis of reality into something "amenable"; this is irrational. Hence, throughout the history of styles and of poets, the irrational dominates. "A Collect of Philosophy" (1951)[42] resumes the business of distinguishing between poetry and philosophy, and concludes that the greatness of poetry may be predicated as the final measure of the stature of modern man, "as if his willingness to believe beyond belief was what had made him modern and was always certain to keep him so." "Two or Three Ideas" (1951)[43] is valuable for its treatment of several basic themes: the power of poetry to convey "the freshness of a world"; its right to be "gaudy"; its replacing of the gods. "In an age of disbelief, when the gods have come to an end, when we think of them as the aesthetic projections of a time that has passed, men turn to a fundamental glory of their own and from that create a style of bearing themselves in reality." The poet's "revelations of reality," which are the new gods, change as reality changes; but they are "items of ecstasy" here and now, not in a place "loftier and more secluded." Of this intensely poetic performance it is even more difficult than usual to give a summary notion; it is one of the finest of Stevens' essays. Of the remaining shorter pieces in *Opus Posthumous* I can say no more than that the short pieces called "Honors and Acts"[44] are important.

One is left, after a reading of the prose, with the sense that one has assisted at the process of thinking rather than that one has heard doctrine preached. Nevertheless, Stevens on the imagination, on religion, on style, on the kind of image that is the basis of more explicitly poetic meditation elsewhere, has in the end perhaps more clarity because the presiding personality is that of a poet and not of a temporary aesthetician. At all events the prose makes clearer a difference between him and his great contemporaries which all their agreements (and they are many) cannot obscure. Yeats, for example, could not have borne this labour to deprive the world of gods, to give it the brilliance of every paradise; he sought no victory over the incredible; not, anyway, the kind of victory Stevens could approve. In an age of poetic myth-making Stevens is almost alone in his respect for those facts which seem "in disconnexion, dead and spiritless."

REFERENCES

1. *O.P.*, pp. 157–80. Morse prints 290 adages from the original notebook. Some had previously appeared as "Materia Poetica" in *View* (1940, 1942).
2. *O.P.*, p. 174.
3. "Esthétique du Mal," xi, *C.P.*, p. 322.
4. *O.P.*, p. 160.
5. *O.P.*, p. 175.
6. *O.P.*, p. 178; p. 165. Cf. "Final Soliloquy of the Interior Paramour," *C.P.*, p. 524; *N.S.F.*, I. i, *C.P.*, p. 380.
7. Preface to *O.P.*, p. xxxiii.
8. "The Noble Rider and the Sound of Words," *N.A.*, pp. 3–36.
9. The first two examples are in "A Collect of Philosophy," *O.P.*, pp. 194, 195; the third in "I.V.," *N.A.*, p. 138; the fourth in "A Collect," *O.P.*, p. 192.
10. "A Collect," *O.P.*, p. 197.
11. In *Adagia*, "A Collect," "F.Y.V.P.," etc.
12. *Vie des Formes* (1947). See "F.Y.V.P.," pp. 46, 48.
13. See the Prefaces to *Eupalinos* and *L'Ame et la Danse*. Stevens' anti-intellectualism is of the same cast as Valéry's; Valéry has similar ideas on "ignorance"; on unparaphrasability; on "accuracy"; on what Stevens calls the *mundo* of poetry; on the relation of the language of poetry to the *lingua franca*, etc.
14. *N.A.*, pp. 147–8.
15. *C.P.*, pp. 508 ff. Other examples of indebtedness to Santayana are given in notes.
16. *Les deux Sources de la morale et de la réligion* (1933), Ch. II.
17. "Esthétique du Mal," iii, *C.P.*, p. 315.
18. "Two or Three Ideas," *O.P.*, p. 213.
19. *O.E.N.H.*, xii, *C.P.*, p. 473. See Ch. V, n. 50.
20. *Adagia*, *O.P.*, p. 169: "The acquisitions of poetry are fortuitous; *trouvailles*. (Hence its disorder.)"
21. *N.S.F.*, III. x, *C.P.*, p. 407. It is something of a favourite word; see *N.S.F.*, I. vi (*C.P.*, p. 385) and "Prologues to What is Possible," *C.P.*, p. 517.
22. "The Irrational Element in Poetry," *O.P.*, p. 217.
23. Introduction to *N.A.*, p. vii.
24. See *N.S.F.*, I. ii, *C.P.*, p. 381, and "The Hermitage at the Centre," *C.P.*, p. 505.
25. *O.E.N.H.*, xii, *C.P.*, p. 474.
26. "The Relations between Poetry and Painting," *N.A.*, p. 175.
27. *N.S.F.*, II. x, *C.P.*, pp. 397–8.
28. "R.P.P.," p. 174.
29. "Angel Surrounded by Paysans," *C.P.*, pp. 496–7.

30. Morse, "The Native Element," pp. 453–6.
31. *N.A.*, Introduction, p. viii.
32. The text of *N.A.* (p. 28) has "readers."
33. See note 23 above.
34. *N.A.*, pp. 39–67.
35. Cf. *N.S.F.*, I. vii: "It feels good as it is without the giant . . ." (*C.P.*, p. 386); and Wordsworth, *Preface to Lyrical Ballads*, for a similar argument.
36. *N.A.*, pp. 71–89.
37. Above, p. 27.
38. *N.A.*, pp. 107–30.
39. *N.A.*, pp. 133–56.
40. *N.A.*, pp. 159–76.
41. *O.P.*, pp. 216–29. The dating is Morse's and is presumably based on the vague "ten or more years ago" of p. 221; it seems to me too early.
42. *O.P.*, pp. 183–202.
43. *O.P.*, pp. 202–216.
44. *O.P.*, pp. 235–47.

CHAPTER V

TRANSPORT TO SUMMER, THE AURORAS OF AUTUMN

Transport to Summer (1947) and *The Auroras of Autumn* (1950) contain between them eighty-nine poems; his sixties were Stevens' most prolific period. The sheer profusion of the verse has been a deterrent to commentators, and has not encouraged readers to abandon *Harmonium* as the focus of their interest in Stevens; O'Connor expresses a rather widely-held opinion when he speaks of the poet's having developed a verse form "suitable to expository writing" and an interest in certain "generalized themes" which invite "over-extension and an element of vagueness."[1] This might be stated less pejoratively: Stevens had developed to an extraordinary degree a manner of commenting upon the text of reality and also upon the commentary which, he said, was equally a part of the real. Each of his poems stands to the others as every poem stands to an inaccessible central poem in which the "incessant conjunctionings" of imagination and reality are brought to a full close: "One poem proves another and the whole."[2] The study of reality produces certain images; these images are meditated;[3] and so habitual and fluent was this meditation that good poems became, at last, almost easy to write. Many of them, for all their fluency, are very obscure, because it never seemed to Stevens part of his job to give us easy access to his *mundo*; the giant mutters and we listen as we wish. "One does not write for any reader except one."[4] A poet who writes in this way is, one would have thought, in some danger of sliding into a dwarfish mumble without knowing it; but it is never safe to lose patience with these poems. The first in *Transport to Summer*, "God is Good. It is a Beautiful Night," may at one reading seem a tiresomely fortuitous collection of props; one may fall into the mistake of reading it as a surrealist poem, as a kind of art that "invents without discovering."[5] But from inside the Stevens world one sees the concordance of the objects: the moon and the zither of imagination, the scholar at his book "hot for another accessible bliss,"[6] the summer of sufficiency at its end; all these images in a brown and valedictory light, disject but capable of concord. The poem is one more unimaginably different repetition, and so illustrates that law also, a law of both the real and the fictive worlds. Stevens states it in a light epigram (*C.P.*, p. 353):

> The romance of the precise is not the elision
> Of the tired romance of imprecision.
> It is the ever-never-changing same,
> An appearance of Again, the diva-dame.

There is little sign that the *fonction fabulatrice* diminished in force; the strangeness of the fable blends perfectly with a familiar theme in "The Good Man has no Shape" (*C.P.*, p. 364), in the lovely and unexpected third poem of "Certain Phenomena of Sound" (*C.P.*, p. 287), in the Lewis Carroll language of "Analysis of a Theme" (*C.P.* p. 348). The originality of "Flyer's Fall" is that of a Stevens commonplace. "Perhaps," as we read near the end of *Notes toward a Supreme Fiction*,

> The man-hero is not the exceptional monster,
> But he that of repetition is most master.[7]

The poems of these volumes are all repetitive in the sense that they are all about some aspect of the Supreme Fiction; about, in other words, the "essential poem" which is the full union of imagination and reality, man satisfied with the world as it is, happy with his beliefs because believing only in the possible. The major effort to get close to this central poem (which has, since it deals in fact, to contain the reasons why one can't ever get close to it) is made in certain longer works; and I propose to deal first with some of the minor poems as tributary to these, and then to speak briefly of five major poems, ignoring chronology by treating *Notes*, the most important, last, not first. For the enjoyment of *Notes* is almost the last reward of a reader's willingness to be acclimatised in the *mundo* of this poet.

The shorter poems are here treated briefly, and I fear crudely, in that I have to emphasise their doctrinal content in a way that falsifies them—they do not make philosophical propositions nakedly—but contaminate metaphysics with fortuity and fable. Also, I lump the two volumes together, though there is a difference of tone, virtually a seasonal difference, as the titles suggest.

When Stevens calls the mind "the most terrible force in the world," he means by "mind" intellect. When he adds that the mind "is also the only force that defends us against terror," he means by "mind" imagination. The adage is the starting-point of "Saint John and the Back-Ache" (*C.P.*, p. 436), in which the acts of imagination are represented as helping us to "face the dumb-foundering abyss | Between us and the object, external cause." They are "The little ignorance that is everything." The "ignorance" of the poet is for Stevens, as for Valéry, Yeats, and Eliot, his defence against intellect, his stand on imagination. The moon, his planet, is "queen of ignorance."[8] He has to evade the categorisations of intellect (which falsify reality, as Bergson held); he must "become an ignorant man again."[9] In this ignorance he fulfils not a personal need ("Poetry is not personal"[10]) but the need of the common imagination. He is in a way anonymous. An inferior poet is called "an obstruction, a man | Too exactly himself."

> there are words
> Better without an author, without a poet,
> Or having a separate author, a different poet,
> An accretion from ourselves, intelligent
> Beyond intelligence.

It is a bad poem that does not "make the visible a little hard | to see." We do not in poems, speak out of our own characters; "We say ourselves in syllables that rise | From the floor, rising in speech we do not speak."[11] The poem that results "must resist the intelligence | Almost successfully."[12] Only thus, in an ascendancy of imaginaton over intellect, can reality be truly seen.

Reality has, therefore, to be imagined: "the absence of the imagination had | Itself to be imagined."[13] The need for this primary act of imagination is imperative:

> It is here, in this bad, that we reach
> The last purity of the knowledge of good.[14]

There is no summer satisfaction without a clear winter apprehension of the need that has to be satisfied. We must know reality as the "myth before the myth began,"[15] we must "accept the structure | Of things as the structure of ideas."[16] We must also remember that, however enormous our effort to bring the great adjective of the poem to this primordial noun, the relation of subject to object is never such that the latter can be fully and finally apprehended. "If the day writhes, it is not with revelations. | One goes on asking questions."

> It would be enough,
> If we were ever, just once, at the middle, fixed
> In This Beautiful World Of Ours and not as now,
>
> Helplessly at the edge, enough to be
> Complete, because at the middle, if only in sense,
> And in that enormous sense, merely enjoy.[17]

This desire is at the root of the "incessant conjunction-ings"; but since reality and the observer alter their mutual stance, change is part of the human condition, and is—must be—accepted and enjoyed for itself. We find

> The obscure moon lighting an obscure world
> Of things that would never be quite expressed,
> Where you yourself were never quite yourself
> And did not want nor have to be,

> Desiring the exhilaration of changes:
> The motive for metaphor, shrinking from
> The weight of primary noon,
> The A B C of being.[18]

Metaphor is an addition to "primary noon," transient and fictive; but "The real" is "made more acute by an un-real."[19] What we say about reality is what makes it as it is. "The theory of description matters most. | It is the theory of the word for those | For whom the word is the making of the world."

> It is a world of words to the end of it,
> In which nothing solid is its solid self.

Description, in this sense, is "the difference that we make in what we see."[20] Consequently, "things seen are things as seen";[21] it is not a long step from "The Emperor of Ice-Cream" (*C.P.*, p. 64)—"let be be finale of seem"—to

> The sun is an example. What it is seems
> It is and in such seeming all things are—[22]

or to the opening of *Notes*.

Such "seemings"—unless we can imagine "a change immenser than | A poet's metaphors,"[23] and that would be the Supreme Fiction—are not constant; the pressure

of reality, the answering force of imagination, vary, and
"the integrations of the past are . . . so much, | So little
our affair, which is the affair | of the possible: seemings
that are to be."[24] Perhaps we should like to know what
reality would be if we could stop our hearts from beating
and, "released from destruction, | To be a bronze man
breathing under archaic lapis . . . at the azury centre of
time";[25] but our affair is with the possible, with a paradise that is, if anywhere, here, with death as a part of life.
The imagination of the poet deals in the final uncer-
tainties, the "confusions of intelligence," by means of
"the formulations of midnight"—and this places him in
total contrast to the priests with their "ever-living subject."[26]

We know from the prose what must be asked of the
imagination, why it is needed as we confront the sea of
reality, "insolid rock," "that which could not be fixed."[27]
We hope to feel "the imagination's mercies."[28] We hope
it will meet with its "ugly lord," reality, and create "the
savage transparence."[29] In a bad time, it recognises and
accepts our poverty, which is that of the beggar:

> What has he? What he has he has. But what? . . .
> What has he that becomes his heart's strong core?
>
> He has his poverty and nothing more.
> His poverty becomes his heart's strong core—
> A forgetfulness of summer at the pole.[30]

At this time it is our only defence against poverty: "he |
That has lost the folly of the moon becomes | The prince
of the proverbs of pure poverty."[31] Seeking what will
suffice, it aims at transformation, apotheosis. Stevens'
"Pastoral Nun"[32] believes "poetry and apotheosis are
one" and outlines the Supreme Fiction as the means of
apotheosis. What she says is, in fact, an allusion to much
of the material in *Notes*:

If I live according to this law I live
In an immense activity, in which

Everything becomes morning, summer, the hero,
The enraptured woman, the sequestered night,
The man that suffered, lying there at ease.

Imagination produces those "momentary harmonies"
which, in the words of Santayana, "bring to a focus the
various impulses of the self, so as to suspend them in a
single image, that a great peace falls upon that perturbed
kingdom."[33] It is at such moments that the poet might
say, "I have | No need, am happy, forget need's golden
hand, | Am satisfied without solacing majesty. . . . I have
not but I am and as I am, I am."[34] If it can take us out of
poverty and into this content, we may well say that
"Poetry is a means of redemption."[35]

The human power that makes these things possible is
considered, in abstraction, as the hero, that aspect of
men which is "miraculous man."[36] As a figure of nobility
this hero can be obsolete, as we saw in "The Noble
Rider" and elsewhere; this obsolete hero recurs in "In the
Element of Antagonisms" (*C.P.*, p. 425). Indeed, the
description of the hero in his relations with men and with
reality turns out to be a difficult and endless task. In
"Chocorua to its Neighbor" (*C.P.*, p. 296) he is "men
without reference to their form," "the self of selves," blue
as ice, strong, "as tall as a tree in the middle of | The
night." He is "Both substance and non-substance," "not
man yet . . . nothing else." He speaks: "My solitaria |
Are the meditations of a central mind." Reality is his
"own voice speaking in his ear." And in that reality

>   lies the misery, the coldest coil
>   That grips the centre, the actual bite, that life
>   Itself is like a poverty in the space of life.

But in spite of this apprehension of poverty he produces

"radiance." He looks out in darkness, "part | Thereof and part desire and part the sense | Of what men are." And, "safely under roof"—that is, within the limits of human perception[37]—are aspects of him: the soldier, the religious, the scholar, "true transfigurers." The giant is human:

> To say more than human things with human voice,
> That cannot be; to say human things with more
> Than human voice, that, also, cannot be;
> To speak humanly from the height or from the depth
> Of human things, that is acutest speech.

This speech is the giant's; and without stepping outside what is human he gives us air to breathe, recreates us, fulfils our desires. He is the prince of "human realizings."

"Chocorua" is not one of the better poems, and moves too slowly. "Repetitions of a Young Captain" (*C.P.*, p. 306) is on the whole even less successful, though its conclusion has some of the passion of *Notes*. That the "major man" is both actual and abstract is the theme of "Paisant Chronicle" (*C.P.*, p. 334): though "fictive" and "artificial," he is "Nothing in which it is not possible | To believe," and you can see him for yourself:

> He may be seated in
> A café. There may be a dish of country cheese
> And a pineapple on the table. It must be so.

His task is the fiction; the reconciliation of the opposites, reality and the mind, to produce "a world that shrinks to an immediate whole."[38] This he has to do among the unhappy, in the world as it is, not as it might be:

> he meditates a whole,
> The full of fortune and the full of fate,
> As if he lived all lives.[39]

This somewhat indigestible extract of ideas from the minor poems in *Transport to Summer* and *Auroras of Autumn* will, I hope, supply the gist of further meditation on the nature of the imaginative fiction and of the mental power that makes it; and we can go on to the longer poems.

Stevens, more than most poets perhaps, needs the power "to confer his identity on the reader."[40] This is because he is so preoccupied with the vistas of his own world, so devoted to his own dialect. In some very long runs, these landscapes are of our world rather than the moon, and those words are kin to the gibberish of the vulgate.[41] If a reader finds the run too long, Stevens allows him to drop out; but in the end his whole theory of poetry resembles those of other post-Symbolist poets in that it provides for communication of meaning, either above or below the level of intellect. And his own provision depends upon this conferment of identity, this power to make a reader at home with the presiding personality and the personal geometry of a *mundo*. There can be no doubt that long poems exercise this power better than short ones; "anyone who has read a long poem day after day as, for example, *The Faerie Queene*, knows how the poem comes to possess the reader and how it naturalizes him in its own imagination and liberates him there."[42] Stevens, I think, succeeded fully in this act of possession only once, in *Notes*. But I deal first with some of the other important longer poems in these volumes.

"Esthétique du Mal" (*C.P.*, p. 313) is an ambitious poem on a subject of great importance to Stevens; it is about the acceptance of evil in reality, and the discovery "in this bad," of "The last purity of the knowledge of good."[43] "The very title . . . indicates clearly the location of positive evil in the texture of reality, the texture which is the stuff of esthetic experience."[44] Hearing Vesuvius groan, the poet in Naples, though pleasantly situated, imaginatively transforms the sound into human pain: "This is a part of the sublime | From which we shrink"—

the knowledge that pain is specifically human. This pain, the second section explains, is "indifferent to the sky," the product of the imagination in conjunction with reality—a conjunction only men can make. In sect. iii, "his firm stanzas" may refer to Dante, who filled Hell with pain; we must see it as part of Earth. The myth of a suffering and merciful God makes this difficult; his pity "relieve[s] us of woe," and generates self-pity; otherwise we might accept the world whole, "the honey of common summer | Might be enough," and pain, made thoroughly human, might be borne. Evil is (sect. iv) part of ourselves, "from which | In desperate hallow, rugged gesture, fault | Falls out on everything." Human love (sect. v), "exquisite in poverty," ought to be without "the inventions of sorrow." Imperfection is (sect. vi) in the nature of reality (the sun, pecked at by a great bird, the mind) and the mind is not content with even the brightest landscape; men reject the actual berries in favour of some promised perfection (Heaven) already obsolete. In sect. vii, as elsewhere in Stevens, the wound of the soldier is an emblem of human suffering and death, "good because life was," leading to "deathless rest." Sect. viii stresses the new quality of the pressure of reality which attended the death (by negation) of Satan. "How cold the vacancy | When the phantoms are gone and the shaken realist | First sees reality." But to be a realist—"to see what one sees," and make no allowance for the human impact on reality—is full poverty; the loss of sensibility, the hearing of "one meaning alone, | As if the paradise of meaning ceased | To be paradise." What is needed is (sect. ix) a new chant or incantation that summons up the whole truth, or "Truth's favors sonorously exhibited." In sect. x the theme is of deceptive explanations; for example that the world, being as it is fecund, gross, female (like the *mundo* of the final poem in *Notes*) is therefore necessarily innocent. It is all these things but not innocent; and sect. xi, the heart of the poem and one of Stevens' finest things, is an acceptance of and rejoicing in the bitterness and poverty native to our lives. We must rejoice in it as it is, with its incomprehensible violence and gross disasters; if it were otherwise it would be false. The imagination, the poem, brings this acceptance.

> Natives of poverty, children of malheur,
> The gaiety of language is our seigneur.

Without pain and without the knowledge of evil ("one feels its action moving in the blood"), the world would be (sect. xii) nothing we know about or love. To abstract from this whole that includes evil some limited political system which would save men from the physical life that includes evil and let them live content in a world of ideas is (sect. xiv) the hope only of "logical lunatics," of revolutionaries who ignore wholeness. For (sect. xv)

> The greatest poverty is not to live
> In a physical world. . . .
> 　　　　　　　Perhaps,
> After death, the non-physical people, in paradise,
> Itself non-physical, may, by chance, observe
> The green corn gleaming and experience
> The minor of what we feel.

Similarly, the dead of an imaginary paradise are called down (as in "Large Red Man reading") to support the thesis that only in the sense of the wholeness and completeness of life, which includes pain, can paradise be found, "completely physical in a physical world," a matter of the August heat, of the "selves" and the "sensuous worlds" we create, "Merely in living as and where we live."

"Esthétique du Mal" lacks the emotional progression that one senses, however obscurely, in *Notes*; and it has moments when the metaphysic and the fable, the idea and the image, seem to jostle each other. But in its great moments, in sects. iii, vi, vii, x, and notably in sects. xi

H　　　　　　　　　　　　　　　　　　　　W.S.

and xv, it has the sure-footed, unpredictable power of Stevens when he moves in his own direction over unfamiliar roads; an authority unique in twentieth-century poetry.

"Credences of Summer" (*C.P.*, p. 372) is no longer than several other poems I have not singled out. It is an example of that incantatory power, the tone of rapture, Stevens sometimes brings to meditation, and is undoubtedly one of his great poems. The subject is total satisfaction, the moment of total summer. "The roses are heavy with a weight | Of fragrance and the mind lays by its trouble." The poem attempts to abstract from this fullness the idea of it, "its essential barrenness,"

> And fill the foliage with arrested peace,
> Joy of such permanence, right ignorance
> Of change still possible. Exile desire
> For what is not.

Green is the colour of reality, and this is "green's green apogee"; here the conjunction of desire and the object is fullest: "happiest folk-land, mostly marriage-hymns." It is a land "too ripe for enigmas"—"we accept what is | As good." This is the strong-point of the year, and of human life. As an emblem of satisfaction there is the rock, half of it covered in blossom, half of it in the light of the "central sky" "the visible rock, the audible, | The brilliant mercy of a sure repose." And this certainty—the paradise of living as and where one lives—is available only to those who fully accept reality, and, possessing the object, subject it to "savage scrutiny"—not to those who evade it, "Deep in the woods" instead of in the sun. For this new total reality succeeds the old myths of invisible fruition; "what is possible | Replaces what is not." Reality, "not part of the listener's own sense," is the bird of sect. ix surveying an allegorical garden where the old arrangements have decayed and made way for natural growth, "salacious weeds," a less "civil" complex. The final section reverts to summer and its satisfied characters,

> Complete in a completed scene, speaking
> Their parts as in a youthful happiness.

There is nothing novel in "Credences" except in the re-imagining of the ideas; its world is the world of "Sunday Morning," but the woman's longing for another life is burned away in the passionate celebration of this August heat.

The theme of *A Primitive like an Orb* (*C.P.*, p. 440) is that possible "degree of perception at which what is real and what is imagined are one: a state of clairvoyant observation, accessible or possibly accessible to the poet or, say, the acutest poet."[45] It is about "the essential poem at the centre of things" and the man, or the power, that makes it. This poem is what makes life good; but it is "a difficult apperception," delicate, achieved by such fleeting and intangible means. We know of it not directly but through "lesser poems." "It is the huge high harmony that sounds | A little and a little, suddenly"—it "captives the being," then disappears. But that captivity is the land of milk and honey. The other poems prove it "for the clairvoyant men . . . the lover, the believer and the poet." They celebrate it in "the joy of language." In the union between man and the world both are changed; the central poem and the world are the same thing, "denouncing separate selves." The other poems are children of this one. Its brilliance is a brilliance of earth, not heaven. It is the strength of the world, a principle and a meditation on the principle, "an inherent order." It is strength, beneficence and repose; it is gay and fortuitous, yet "vested in the serious folds of majesty." It is a giant, "a close, parental magnitude . . . prodigious person, patron of origins." All that the lover, the believer, the poet and the painter know is the part accessible to each of "the giant of nothingness . . . the giant ever changing, living in change."

An Ordinary Evening in New Haven (C.P., p. 465) is a set of thirty-one meditations, each of six three-line stanzas, on a topic announced in the opening lines:

> The eye's plain version is a thing apart,
> The vulgate of experience. Of this,
> A few words, an and yet, and yet, and yet—
>
> As part of the never-ending meditation,
> Part of the question that is a giant himself.

The clue to this poem is in the contemporary lecture "Three Academic Pieces": "What our eyes behold may well be the text of life but one's meditations on the text and the disclosures of these meditations are no less a part of the structure of reality."[46] What the eye sees in New Haven is real, "of the sun"—but so is the contribution of imagination, the second giant, which provides "A recent imagining of reality" that makes a new, a festive, whole. (Note "recent": constant re-imagining is the task of the mind as it defends us against poverty.) The second section supposes the town as we would desire it, formed and coloured by the human mind, "object | Of the perpetual meditation, point | Of the enduring, visionary love," part of ourselves. Such a creation comes (sect. iii) of the desire of the mind that cannot be satisfied or frustrated because it can never possess. But (sect. iv) the desire to accommodate the "savagery" of "plain things" is assuaged by a matching and mating the opposites, "a savage and subtle and simple harmony," as "lewd spring comes from winter's chastity." The division that makes these opposites occurs (sect. v) in the self of man; and he therefore labours to reconcile them, common earth and central sky, seeking "majesty" in his "moonlit extensions." In sect. vi, Reality is Alpha, re-imaginings of it Omega; the one unchanging, the other constantly refreshed. ("The real is only the base. But it is the base."[47]) These inventions (sect. vii) make men richer, more alive, make them come closer to a gay truth about themselves. Our longing for the real is (sect. viii) of our nature; it is a desire to speak "the syllable | Of recognition," the "cry that contains its converse in itself"—the word of imagination that contains reality. We return not to old and obsolete integrations ("hymns") but to reality itself, seeking "the poem of pure reality, untouched | By trope."[48] We seek nothing (sect. ix) *beyond* reality; but *all* that it includes— "the spirit's alchemicana"—is part of what we seek: the comment as well as the text. Away from home (sect. x), in the moon for instance,[49] we should lack power, but on earth we know our environment, the enigmas of our own reality; we can live with gaiety "in a permanence composed of impermanence." We must live (sect. xi) with New Haven as it is, metaphysical and physical at once, in the light of day; though in need of majesty we must be free of false majesty, propounding the minimum fiction, that of the brilliant earth. The poem is (sect. xii) a part of reality here and now,[50] as it is; the agent of order, "the life of the world." The young poet knows (sect. xiii) of the need for "a fresh spiritual"—he must abstract, seek out the cold idea hidden in the stale warmth of dead beliefs; he deals with New Haven, "the actual landscape with its actual horns | Of baker and butcher," not with Paradise. Sect. xiv introduces Professor Eucalyptus; the eucalyptus tree desires water and seeks God in a rainy cloud, but the Professor's desires compel him with equal thirst to seek God in the object as it really is. The only choice he has is a choice of adjective, of description; "for what he sees, it comes in the end to that: | The description that makes it divinity." The whole of what he sees must get into his description; for instance, rain in a broken spout. He leaves this out (sect. xv) only because of its correspondence to his deepest, least accessible self,

that dryness which will only be satisfied when his en-
environment becomes his total world, "In which he is
and as and is are one." Sect. xvi I find difficult; it stresses,
like II. i of *Notes*, the novelty of each new repetition (here
of the dawn) and seems to speak of this as a possible cue
for meditation on the individual death. Sect. xvii, however, rejects both the tragic and the comic as final com-
ment: "The serious reflection is composed | Neither of
comic nor tragic but of commonplace," the ordinary evening in New Haven. The difficulty is (sect. xviii) to achieve
this: to be absolutely in the present, as art needs to be,
and not hankering after the dead past. As the moon (for
Stevens as for Coleridge the imagination's planet) unifies
by its light, so (sect. xix) at all times, including the present, an order, a central controlling image is possible.
What is it in this place? The hero will answer, but obscurely. The town (sects. xx–xxi) is merely the base of
imaginative activity, the human finding what will suffice.
Professor Eucalyptus, says the poet (sect. xxii), searches
for the "first idea,"[51] the abstract "of original cold | And
of original earliness," in order to re-create it, exploring
the possibleness of a possible, nor of a comforting dream.
The sun of day creates our "separate, several selves," but
night (the moon) recomposes them. Sect. xxiv allegorises
the moment of possible apotheosis, "An escape from
repetition, a happening | In space and the self, that
touched them both at once." The hero, given (sect. xxv)
his guitar, is he who makes "the commonplace . . . a
rumpling of blazons," turns the real into "something
most unreal," and ends isolation. In sect. xxvi there is a
contrast between reality seen through a bogus rhetoric,
distanced by deceit, and the real thing in its poverty,
formless, but to be loved. Sect. xxvii is another version of
the now familiar hero, "consort of the Queen of Fact,"
abolishing "That which is not ourselves"; with his queen
he "lies at his ease beside the sea." In sect. xxviii, "Real
and unreal are two in one," because reality exists in the

mind; the theory of poetry is the life of poetry, and the
theory of poetry is the theory of life;[52] out of its metaphors and its "as-ifs" (the whole poem is full of "as-ifs")
are created "The heavens, the hells, the worlds, the
longed-for lands". The fable of sect. xxix illustrates the
impact of description on reality, "an alteration | Of words
that was a change of nature." In sect. xxx there is
another familiar topic; the return to the plain sense of
things when the summer of re-imagining is over; a new
act of abstraction, a necessary new winter clarity. And
the last stanza describes the return of the myriad agents
of re-imagining, "edgings and inchings of final form,"
the mind once more in search of what will suffice.

An Ordinary Evening is full of superb *trouvailles*, the fortuitous caught up into and sustained in meditation; its
maintenance of a central theme, the endless freshnesses
of the vocabulary of its repetitions, compensate one for
the sense that one is never quite heartily admitted to the
town or given a share in the fables. The persistence of its
metaphysics tends to reduce the brilliance it ought to
have as kin, however poor, of the Supreme Fiction; it
is not quite living in a physical world. This is one of the
ways in which it falls short of *Notes*, the last topic of this
chapter.

I will not disgrace Stevens' greatest poem by plodding
commentary. There is no metaphysical theme in *Notes*[53]
that has not already been discussed in relation to other
poems, and the need is now to sense the immanence of
such themes. In such a poem "the feeling of one man is
communicated to another in words of the exquisite appo-
siteness that takes away all their verbality."[54] Comment
puts the "verbality" back in; the clearer the explanations,
the falser they are likely to be. (It is worth recalling that
accurate aphorism, "Poetry must resist the intelligence
almost successfully.")[55] Sometimes what is being explained isn't even fully there; Stevens is always fantastic,
and when he creates a nature, as he does in *Notes*, it is

shown as if in continous creation, changing and incomplete, so that an image or an idea may be seen like Milton's lion, pawing to get free his hinder parts.

In this poem, as in no other, the fortuitous and the meditative are happy together. The activity of the poet, though familiar, is quite unpredictable; the final poem is a fact not before realised, a contribution to reality. From it ideas of order may be inferred; but it is a nature, not a physics. It is a nature full of the squawk and clatter of birds, of unique flowers, of the excitement of changing seasons, of unexpected persons welling out of the *fonction fabulatrice*, of resemblances, of irrational transitions. It gives us pleasure because of the way we are and because of where we are; because it satisfies our desire to convert our *Lumpenwelt*, the irrational needs of our sensibility. It is true; it deals not with myth but with fact, the fact not realised before. The fiction is the ever-changing truth.

"One poem proves another and the whole." The best preparation for *Notes* is to soak oneself in the *Collected Poems*. But something may be done to aid an unimpeded reading of the poem by explanations of the sectional titles. (All three imperatives are hinted in the little prologue: the truth is single, is perceived as changing, brings peace and pleasure. This poem is, of course, addressed to the "interior paramour." The imagination resembles light in that it falls on reality, "adding nothing but itself.")

It must be Abstract. "Man fabricates by abstraction": Stevens approved the saying of Valéry's Socrates.[56] By "abstraction," as we have seen, Stevens does not mean the falsifications of intellect, described in "Landscape with Boat." Blake's "minute particulars" are of the essence of his "abstract." They have to be abstracted from all the dead formulae that obscure them, to be looked on as a reality free of imaginative (or, since they are obsolete, imaginary) accretions; to be seen absolutely, "without evasion by a single metaphor."[57] This abstracted reality is represented (as in "The Snow Man") by the bare icy

outlines of winter. But after winter, spring: the newly
perceived analogies, related particulars, colours, sounds,
rush in and vanquish—or, in Stevens' word, "vanish"—
the cold outline, satisfying the human need for this union
with the world. The fully re-imagined reality is expressed
as summer, the only paradise, the full satisfaction. With
fall and winter the cycle proceeds. "After the leaves have
fallen we return | To a plain sense of things. It is as if | We
had come to an end of the imagination. . . . Yet the
absence of the imagination had | Itself to be im-
agined. . . ."[58] For all imaginative activity that has a real
relevance to our poverty and need starts from this primary
effort of abstraction. It is a recognition of reality imper-
ceptible except in poems; and the measure of a poet's
power is his ability "to abstract himself, and to withdraw
with him into his abstraction the reality on which the
lovers of truth insist."[59] Thus the cycle runs from abstraction to re-imagining, to loss of power through the "eva-
sions of metaphor," to a renewed effort of abstraction,
and so on (I. iii):

> The poem refreshes life so that we share,
> For a moment, the first idea. . . It satisfies
> Belief in an immaculate beginning
>
> And sends us, winged by an unconscious will,
> To an immaculate end. We move between these points:
> From that ever-early candor to its late plural
>
> And the candor of them is the strong exhilaration
> Of what we feel from what we think, of thought
> Beating in the heart, as if blood newly came,
>
> An elixir, an excitation, a pure power.
> The poem, through candor, brings back a power again
> That gives a candid kind to everything.

The act of imaginative abstraction is primary; on it
depends all re-imagining. The old "integrations" be-

come obsolete; change creates the need for new ones. Consequently the "ephebe"—the young man in receipt of this obscure advice on how to be a hero or a virile poet—must first cleanse the sun, reality, from all mythical accretions. Only thus can we make it available for new and more relevant "plurals," his own fiction.

It must Change. "The imagination . . . generates as well as abstracts," says Santayana in *The Sense of Beauty,* and, again, "It is possible that changes in the character of the facts . . . should necessitate the continual reconstruction of our world."[60] Or, in Stevens' version,

> Why should a poem not change in sense when there is a fluctuation of the whole of appearance? Or why should it not change when we realize that the indifferent experience of life is the unique experience, the item of ecstasy which we have been isolating and reserving for another time and place, loftier and more secluded?[61]

It is this constancy of change that renders obsolete heaven and hell, the myths and the gods.[62] If we could produce any fixed image of the world we should want to call it the chief or only image; and no matter how great and inclusive it might be, it could not content the imagination, the "irrepressible revolutionist."[63] We decreate reality; reduce it to the uncreated, and then make it again, transform it, give it our order (II. x):

> The casual is not
> Enough. The freshness of transformation is
>
> The freshness of a world. It is our own,
> It is ourselves, the freshness of ourselves.

Change, then, is essential to the precious physical reality Stevens sets up against Platonism; it provides the revelations of reality that belong to the merely physical world.

The giant is "ever changing, living in change," and so is the Fiction. The poles of change are the "ever-early candor" of the first idea and its "late plural," the various and fluctuant union of the imagined and the real. Imagination exhausts part of reality,[64] and each new imaginative act is performed on different matter. It is "as if the air, the mid-day air, was swarming | With the metaphysical changes that occur, | Merely in living as and where we live."[65]

"It must Change" consists of parables and illustrations of this theme, relating it to the other two. The statue of General Du Puy, for instance, is an example of the obsolescent noble rider; he does not change, but belongs "among our more vestigial states of mind," and becomes "rubbish in the end" (II. iii). The fourth section is one of Stevens' most ravishing explanations (II. iv):

> Two things of opposite natures seem to depend
> On one another, as a man depends
> On a woman, day on night, the imagined
>
> On the real. This is the origin of change.
> Winter and spring, cold copulars, embrace
> And forth the particulars of rapture come.
>
> Music falls on the silence like a sense,
> A passion that we feel, not understand.
> Morning and afternoon are clasped together
>
> And North and South are an intrinsic couple
> And sun and rain a plural, like two lovers
> That walk away as one in the greenest body.

Out of the "exhilarations of changes"[66] proceed "the particulars of rapture." Consequently the supreme fiction "must give pleasure."

It must give Pleasure. "The purpose of poetry is to con-

tribute to man's happiness."[67] Here Stevens is at one with
Wordsworth and Coleridge, indeed with the whole
Romantic tradition, though closest, perhaps, to the
subtle hedonism of Santayana. "Not until I confound
the impressions and suffuse the symbols themselves
with the emotions they arouse, and find joy and sweet-
ness in the very words I hear, will the expressiveness
constitute beauty; as when they sing, *Gloria in excelsis
Deo*."[68]

It is necessary to extend the sense of "pleasure" to
include other meanings, such as "health" ("Poetry is
a health"[69]); consolation; whatever mitigates the poverty
of the children of malheur. "Pleasure" is the mode of
operation of the one comforter, the gaiety of language.
It is what helps people to live their lives. The poet "has
had immensely to do with giving life whatever savor it
possesses . . . he is an *amoureux perpétuel* of the world that
he contemplates and thereby enriches."[70] His pleasure is
sometimes called a "liberation," or a "justification,"
meaning "a kind of justice of which we had not known
and on which we had not counted," a "purification"; and
in the state of elevation he provides "we feel perfectly
adapted to the idea that moves and *l'oiseau qui chante*."[71]
Even the poet who created God uttered "hymns of joy"
to celebrate his creation. This pleasure is "a pleasure of
agreement with the radiant and productive world"[72] in
which the poet lives. He is the only giver of true pleasure,
since he alone provides, not the obsolete joys of heaven,
but those revelations of reality which proceed from the
"more than rational" apprehension of the physical world.
The first poem of the section insists on the difference between the old customary religious joys, the "jubilas at
exact, accustomed times," and the fortuitous integrations
of the modern giant (III. i):

> the difficultest rigor is forthwith,
> On the image of what we see, to catch from that

Irrational moment its unreasoning,
As when the sun comes rising, when the sea
Clears deeply, when the moon hangs on the wall

Of heaven-haven.[73]

And the final poem celebrates the *mundo* which is the world
so perceived. "In the service of love and imagination
nothing can be too lavish, too sublime or too festive";[74]
so to this theme are devoted the complex splendours of the
fables which bring the poem to an end. These two hundred
lines of verse seem to me to give continuously a higher
delight than anything of comparable length written in
this century.

The imperative "it must give pleasure" is examined
and obeyed throughout Stevens' poems. From "Sunday
Morning" and "Life is Motion" to the confrontation of
pleasure with pain in "Esthétique du Mal" and the
solemn certainties of "Final Soliloquy" the theme persists. But nowhere is the deep movement of the poet's
pleasure so well attested as by the magnificent elevation
of *Notes*, III, where the theme challenged him most directly.

The poem has in each of its three parts ten poems of
seven three-lined stanzas, with a short prelude and a
kind of coda. The three parts lie, as it were, beside each
other; there is no continuous development in the thought.
"Each phase is conceived," as R. P. Blackmur puts it,
"as a version of the other two, that is, with a mutual and
inextricable, rather than with a successive, relationship."[75] Here, as in *A Primitive like an Orb*, Stevens arrives
at a kind of climax (in the thirtieth poem) where he allows
himself a cry of "That's it!" But "it" is a rightness of
feeling, not a claim to have completed a demonstration.
We *"feel* the obscurity of an order,"[76] are content with
"the more than rational distortion, | The fiction that re-
sults from feeling." Order has been discovered in, not imposed upon, the world, and reality completed by the "fictive covering" that "weaves always glistening from the

heart and mind" (II. viii). Yet there is, for all that, a genuine beginning and end, an early candour and a late plural, in the poem. A good deal of the doctrine is contained in the opening poems; and in the final part the fables are used to achieve a deliberate intensity of feeling. The complex and majestic Canon Aspirin poems (from III. v to the opening of III. ix, where the theme modulates into the bird noises picked up again from II. vi) raise the temperature of the whole work and justify not only the sober ecstasies of the conclusion but the immense and beautiful claims for poetry made in III. viii: if the poet creates an angel (and he has just done so) is not his joy equal to the angel's?

> What am I to believe? If the angel in his cloud,
> Serenely gazing at the violent abyss,
> Plucks on his strings to pluck abysmal glory,
>
> Leaps downward through evening's revelations, and
> On his spredden wings, needs nothing but deep space,
> Forgets the gold centre, the golden destiny,
>
> Grows warm in the motionless motion of his flight,
> Am I that imagine this angel less satisfied?
> Are the wings his, the lapis-haunted air?
>
> Is it he or is it I that experience this?
> Is it I then that keep saying there is an hour
> Filled with expressible bliss, in which I have
>
> No need, am happy, forget need's golden hand,
> Am satisfied without solacing majesty,
> And if there is an hour there is a day,
>
> There is a month, a year, there is a time
> In which majesty is a mirror of the self:
> I have not but I am and as I am, I am.

The power of this is great in isolation; in its context, as sequel to the previous poem, it is overwhelming. Yet it is far from being wholly representative of the tone of the poem, which extends from potent argumentation to extraordinary ventriloquial bird-poems, from furious springs to the calm green satisfactions of August. Perhaps of the third part only could it be said that each of the ten poems is a great poem; but the whole work exists in a radiant and productive atmosphere, saying the words of the world that are the life of the world.

REFERENCES

1. O'Connor, *Shaping Spirit*, p. 131.

2. "A Primitive Like an Orb," *C.P.*, p. 441.

3. R. H. Pearce has an excellent passage on "the relationship between the propositions and the poetry" in these volumes; "Wallace Stevens: The Life of the Imagination," pp. 571–2. And see L. Martz, "Wallace Stevens: The World as Meditation," pp. 530 ff. for comparisons between Stevens' meditation and formal religious meditative techniques as used by Donne and Hopkins.

4. *Adagia*, *O.P.*, p. 165.

5. "The essential fault of surrealism," according to Stevens, *Adagia*, *O.P.*, p. 177.

6. *N.S.F.*, II. vii, *C.P.*, p. 395.

7. *N.S.F.*, III. ix, *C.P.*, p. 406.

8. "A Word with José Rodríguez-Feo," *C.P.*, p. 333.

9. *N.S.F.*, I. i, *C.P.*, p. 380. See also the Preface to *Eupalinos*.

10. *Adagia*, *O.P.*, p. 159.

11. "The Creations of Sound," *C.P.*, 310–11.

12. "Man Carrying Thing," *C.P.*, pp. 350–1. Here one of the *Adagia* (*O.P.*, p. 171) is set down intact in the poem and illustrated by a fable; a good simple example of this practice of Stevens.

13. "The Plain Sense of Things," *C.P.*, pp. 502–3. (This poem is in *The Rock*.)

14. "No Possum, No Sop, No Taters," *C.P.*, p. 293.

15. *N.S.F.*, I. iv, *C.P.*, p. 383.

16. "The Bed of Old John Zeller," *C.P.*, pp. 326–7. See Chapter I, pp. 3 ff.

17. "The Ultimate Poem is Abstract," *C.P.*, pp. 429–30.

18. "The Motive for Metaphor," *C.P.*, p. 288. See *N.A.*, p. 77, for a study of

metaphor as a fictive agent.

19. "The Bouquet," iii, *C.P.*, p. 451. See conclusion of "F.Y.V.P.", *N.A.*, p. 67.

20. "Description without Place," *C.P.*, p. 345, p. 344. An important "doctrine" poem.

21. *Adagia*, *O.P.*, p. 162.

22. "Description without Place," *C.P.*, p. 339.

23. "Description without Place," *C.P.*, p. 341.

24. ibid., p. 342.

25. "The Solitude of Cataracts," *C.P.*, p. 425.

26. "Reply to Papini," *C.P.*, p. 446. (A poem of extraordinary brilliance.)

27. "Two Versions of the Same Poem," i, *C.P.*, p. 353, p. 354.

28. "Imago," *C.P.*, p. 439.

29. "The Pediment of Appearance," *C.P.*, p. 361.

30. "In a Bad Time," *C.P.*, 426–7. See also "World without Peculiarity," *C.P.*, pp. 453–4, and "Final Soliloquy," *C.P.*, p. 524.

31. "Esthétique du Mal," ix, *C.P.*, p. 320.

32. "A Pastoral Nun," *C.P.*, p. 378.

33. *The Sense of Beauty* (1896), p. 235.

34. *N.S.F.*, iii. viii, *C.P.*, pp. 404–5.

35. *Adagia*, *O.P.*, p. 160.

36. *Adagia*, *O.P.*, p. 160.

37. This figure occurs also in *Notes*, i. v, i. vii, and iii. viii (*C.P.*, pp. 384, 385,

405). See also "Evening with Angels," *C.P.*, p. 138.

38. "Description without Place," iii, *C.P.*, p. 341.

39. "The Auroras of Autumn," x, *C.P.*, pp. 420–1. For an idea that almost certainly influenced Stevens on "major man," see Santayana, *Three Philosophical Poets* (1910) p. 214–5: "The *altissimo poeta* should live in the continual presence of all experience, and respect it; he should at the same time understand nature, the ground of that experience; and he should also have a delicate sense for the ideal echoes of his own passions, and for all the colors of his possible happiness. . . . But this supreme poet is in limbo still." So Stevens admits that "the great poetry I have projected is a compensation of time to come." ("A Collect of Philosophy," *O.P.*, p. 188).

40. *Adagia*, *O.P.*, p. 158.

41. *N.S.F.*, ii. ix, *C.P.*, p. 396.

42. "F.Y.V.P.," *N.A.*, p. 50. See also "Effects of Analogy," *N.A.*, pp. 111–12.

43. "No Possum, No Sop, No Taters," *C.P.*, p. 293.

44. Pearce, "Wallace Stevens: The Life of the Imagination," p. 576.

45. *Adagia*, *O.P.*, p. 166.

46. *N.A.*, p. 76.

47. *Adagia*, *O.P.*, p. 160.

48. Cf., "Without evasion by a single metaphor," "Credences of Summer," *C.P.*, p. 373.

49. See "N.R.," *N.A.*, p. 8; and "Extracts from Addresses to the Academy of Fine Ideas," vii, *C.P.*, p. 258.

50. Cf. Santayana, "The poem, we can say, may refer to universals as well as particulars, but the universals must exist *in re*, in the concrete experience of the poem, not merely *ante rem* in the mind of the poet or *post rem* in the reflection of the reader." *The Philosophy of George Santayana*, ed. Schilpp (1940), p. 273.

51. *N.S.F.*, i. i, *C.P.*, p. 380.

52. *Adagia*, *O.P.*, p. 178.

53. For commentaries on *Notes*, see R. P. Blackmur, "Wallace Stevens: An Abstraction Blooded," *Form and Value in Modern Poetry*, pp. 213–17; R. H. Pearce, "Wallace Stevens: The Life of the Imagination," Howard Pack, *Wallace Stevens*, B. Heringman, "Wallace Stevens: The Use of Poetry," *E.L.H.*, xvi (1949), pp. 325–36, L. Frankenberg, *The Pleasure Dome* (1949), pp. 257–67.

54. "Effects of Analogy," *N.A.*, p. 118.

55. *Adagia*, *O.P.*, p. 171; "Man Carrying Thing," *C.P.*, pp. 350–1.

56. Preface to *Eupalinos*, p. xiii; *O.P.*, p. 272.

57. "Credences of Summer," ii, *C.P.*, p. 373.

58. "The Plain Sense of Things," *C.P.*, pp. 502–3.

59. "N.R.," *N.A.*, p. 23.

60. Santayana, *The Sense of Beauty*, p. 191.

61. "Two or Three Ideas," *O.P.*, p. 213.

62. See "Two or Three Ideas," "N.R.," "F.Y.V.P."

63. "I.V.," *N.A.*, p. 152.

64. *Adagia*, *O.P.*, p. 173.

65. "Esthétique du Mal," xv, *C.P.*, p. 326.

66. "The Motive for Metaphor," *C.P.*, p. 288.

67. *Adagia*, *O.P.*, p. 168.

68. *The Sense of Beauty*, p. 197.

69. *Adagia*, *O.P.*, p. 176.

70. "N.R.," *N.A.*, p. 30.

71. "F.Y.V.P.," *N.A.*, p. 51.

72. "F.Y.V.P.," *N.A.*, p. 57.

73. The compound word is G. M. Hopkins', which reminds us that Stevens approximates to a secularised version of "inscape."

74. "I.V.," *N.A.*, p. 154.

75. "Wallace Stevens: An Abstraction Blooded," p. 214.

76. "Final Soliloquy of the Interior Paramour," *C.P.*, p. 524.

CHAPTER VI

THE ROCK; LAST POEMS: CONCLUSION

The Rock, the final section of *Collected Poems* (1954), contains twenty-five poems of undiminished power; indeed there is sometimes a hint of a new and moving clarity of expression. Many of these poems must have been written when Stevens was over seventy—indeed they allude more than once to his age. Death and old age, already present in *Harmonium* as necessary parts of the wholeness of life, are now close to the centre. The tone is elegiac, but it remains strong; the elegy is a hymn to physical life, and the great themes of meditation, incessantly repeated, never lose their novelty. "The Hermitage at the Center" (*C.P.*, p. 505), for instance, contrives, by a formal device which is not only original but beautiful, to present a fusion of opposites; bleak winter seems to cancel the summer paradise but really blends with it, and brings together the beginning and the end. There is, says the old poet, a winter difficulty in even choosing "the adjective | For this blank cold";[1] but the difficulty itself is converted into an adjective, a valid description implying wholeness. This is the point of "Long and Sluggish Lines" (*C.P.*, p. 522), a poem about the pre-history of a poem in the seventy-year-old mind; a despair at repetition which gives way to a certainty of freshness yet to come. For the blessedness of change does not falter. The surprising little "Song of Fixed Accord" (*C.P.*, p. 519)—it would not look out of place in *Harmonium*—says that only in the perception of an animal is there an established reality that does not change—the theme of *Notes*, I. v and II. vi. Change will end in death, a matter for grief, but grief is part of the human whole. The dead poet "brings all that he saw into the earth, to the waiting parent"—

> His grief is that his mother should feed on him, him-
>   self and what he saw,
> In that distant chamber, a bearded queen, wicked in
>   her dead light.[2]

He cannot even comfort himself that the "integrations" he achieved have any real permanence; all he can leave is fragments of himself and his work:

> He had said that everything possessed
> The power to transform itself, or else,
>
> And what meant more, to be transformed . . .
>   But his mastery
>
> Left only the fragments found in the grass,
> From his project, as finally magnified.[3]

But the gaiety underlying this elegiac mood is most clearly illustrated in one of the lovely little personal poems of Stevens' final period, "The Planet on the Table" (*C.P.*, p. 532). "Ariel was glad he had written his poems."

> It was not important that they survive.
> What mattered was that they should bear
> Some lineament or character,
>
> Some affluence, if only half-perceived,
> In the poverty of their words,
> Of the planet of which they were part.

The Rock is memorable for such short poems—it includes also "The Final Soliloquy"—but also for three longer poems that deserve to be placed among the best of all Stevens' work, "The World as Meditation," "To an Old Philosopher in Rome," and "The Rock."[4] In the first of these, Penelope desires Ulysses, for his arrival will end all her waiting and bring her full satisfaction. Unlike Nanzia Nunzio in *Notes*, II. viii, passionately desiring an impossible union with an inflexible order, Penelope waits patiently. What comes may be Ulysses, or only the spring sun; yet the spring renewal *is* he, in a sense—all of order that can come, and enough. It is one of the most satisfying of Stevens' fables.

"To an Old Philosopher" proceeds from that veneration for Santayana's life and work which Stevens expressed in "Imagination as Value."[5] Santayana spent his last years in a Roman convent: "in his old age, he dwells in the head of the world." In his failing consciousness, perhaps, he dwells in two worlds, "Rome, and that more merciful Rome | Beyond." The two worlds are the real and the imagined: "How easily the blown banners change to wings. . . ." The philosopher ("impenitent | As to one, and, as to one, most penitent") can speak accurately of them. "Impatient for the grandeur that you need | In so much misery," he finds this grandeur only in the facts of misery, "Profound poetry of the poor and of the dead." Santayana is treated here with the reverence of deep emotion; but the poem is another repetition, another novelty concerning death and "poverty" as part of life.

> It is poverty's speech that seeks us out the most.
> It is older than the oldest speech of Rome.

And the philosopher speaks it, inaudibly, in his room full of known matter-of-fact things, yet charged with "a total grandeur" as the climax of a life constructed like a poem. Considering the grandeur of this structure of Stevens, it is hard to believe that anyone now holds the view that he came to grief a little way on from *Harmonium*.

"The Rock" is based on the symbol first used in "Credences of Summer," vi.[6] A late starter among Stevens' images, it comes to its fullest expression here. Like the tree of Attis' image in Yeats, it represents the reconciliation of opposites; earth and sky, known and unknown:

"half way green and then, | The other immeasurable half,
such rock | As placid air becomes." Like the "self," in
New Haven, v, it has one part that "holds fast tenaciously
in common earth," and one that deals in "moonlit exten-
sions." In sect. i of the new poem the past seems dead and
illusory; but "its permanent cold" bred the desire for
warmth, and this desire covered the rock in green: the
illusion was "like a blindness cleaned." The second, certainly one of the great poems, stems from the adage,
"Poetry is a cure of the mind."[7] The final cure for the
poverty of reality is death . . . and yet the poem might be
the cure, too, the new leaves on the rock might medicine us.

> The fiction of the leaves is the icon
>
> Of the poem, the figuration of blessedness,
> And the icon is the man.

The poem is ourselves; we cover the rock, fill it with
meanings "Of such mixed motion and such imagery |
That its barrenness becomes a thousand things | And so
exists no more." The rock, in the final section, is "the
starting point of the human and the end"; but between
these points the day lights it, and the night of imagination
also, with "its midnight-minting fragrances." "The Rock"
is in Stevens' religious mode; curiously, the opening four
lines of the sect. ii strongly recall Eliot, a poet Stevens
had not formerly found very sympathetic.

> It is not enough to cover the rock with leaves.
> We must be cured of it by a cure of the ground
> Or a cure of ourselves, that is equal to a cure
>
> Of the ground, a cure beyond forgetfulness.

In *Opus Posthumous* is a last handful of poems written
after *The Rock.* The pattern of repetition and novelty is
maintained. One grandly original variation on a familiar
theme has a punning title that contains much of what I
call Stevens' "physics": "Reality is an Activity of the

Most August Imagination" (*O.P.*, p. 110). In "Local Objects" (*O.P.*, p. 111) the subject is again the man or poet concerned with "objects not present as a matter of course . . . the few things | For which a fresh name always occurred."

> He wanted to make them, keep them from perishing,
> The few things, the objects of insight, the integrations
> Of feeling, the things that came of their own accord—

on the days, that is, when reality arranged itself as a poem, and the concrete particulars, freshly abstracted as such, gave evidence of a new idea of order. What was perhaps Stevens' last poem, "A Mythology reflects its Region,"[8] asks, in its ten lines, most of the familiar, repetitious, ever-changing questions, and provides the fully personal answer:

> The image must be of the nature of its creator.
> It is the nature of its creator increased,
> Heightened. It is he, anew, in a freshened youth
> And it is he in the substance of his region,
> Wood of his forests and stone out of his fields
> Or from under his mountains.

Reality is the world seen for a moment whole and happy on an ordinary evening in Hartford.

"Seek those purposes," Stevens advised himself, "that are purely the purposes of the pure poet."[9] Much commentary on the activity that resulted is bound to give the impression that this kind of pure poetry carries badly-made bundles of ideas on its back. But it is genuinely the poetry of a man who thought poetry began where philosophy left off. If "poetry is an instrument of the will to perceive the innumerable accords . . . that make life a thing different from what it would be without such insights,"[10] then it is the business of thinking men. "The greater the mind the greater the poet . . . the poet does his job by virtue of an effort of the mind."[11] His fictions may result from feeling; but thought is felt. The poet's business is not merely to satisfy the lovers of truth, but to make brilliant the poverty on which their thoughts dwell. By altering the world he makes it acceptable to humanity.[12]

None of the thinking that goes to the provision of this sufficiency can be extracted from the poems and judged as philosophy. The thinking is part of the fiction. It is as much altered in the poems as any other fact: the immense dew of Florida, or the woman singing at Key West. When comment is so difficult there is much to be said for the bold simplicity with which Mr Martz states the theme of Stevens' meditation: "attentive thinking about concrete things with the aim of developing an affectionate understanding of how good it is to be alive."[13] In the end that is the subject of Stevens: living without God and finding it good, because of the survival of the power that once made Him suffice.

The degree of attention to reality, the faithfulness of mind he required of poets, has rarely been so unflaggingly exercised as by Stevens. He made his world, his analogue of reality,[14] habitable, not only by his powers of "transference," but also by the patient charting of it, so that we come to know it as the Chinese know their Chinese gods. As to the relation between *Harmonium*, the preliminary survey, and the rest of his explorations, it could not be better described than in words Stevens himself quotes from Focillon:

A vocation recognizes its material by foresight, before experience. As an example of this, [Focillon] refers to the first state of the *Prisons* of Piranesi as skeletal. But "twenty years later, Piranesi returned to these etchings, and on taking them up again, he poured into them shadow after shadow, until one might say that he excavated this astonishing darkness not from the brazen plates, but from the living rock of some subterranean world."[15]

REFERENCES

1. "The Plain Sense of Things," *C.P.*, p. 502.

2. "Madame La Fleurie," *C.P.*, p. 507.

3. "Two Illustrations that the World is what you make of it," ii, *C.P.*, pp. 514–15.

4. *C.P.*, pp. 520–1, 508–11, 525–8.

5. *N.A.*, pp. 147–8.

6. *C.P.*, p. 375. See also *O.P.*, p. 241, *C.P.*, p. 476, *N.A.*, p. viii.

7. *Adagia*, *O.P.*, p. 176.

8. *O.P.*, p. 118. Cf. this remarkable statement: "One turns with something like ferocity toward a land that one loves, to which one is really and essentially native, to demand that it surrender, reveal, that in itself which one loves. This is a vital affair, not an affair of the heart (as it may be in one's first poems), but an affair of the whole being (as in one's last poems), a fundamental affair of life, or, rather, an affair of fundamental life." ("John Crowe Ransom: Tennessean," [1948], *O.P.*, p. 260.)

9. *Adagia*, *O.P.*, p. 157.

10. *O.P.*, p. 242.

11. "R.P.P.," *N.A.*, p. 165.

12. See "Extracts from Addresses to the Academy of Fine Ideas," vii, *C.P.*, p. 257.

13. "Wallace Stevens: The World as Meditation," pp. 532–3.

14. "... a transcendent analogue composed of the particulars of reality, created by the poet's sense of the world." ("Effects of Analogy," *N.A.*, p. 130.)

15. "F.Y.V.P.," *N.A.*, pp. 48–9.

BIBLIOGRAPHY

NOTE (1967)

Many books and articles on Stevens have appeared since the first publication of this study. In the Addenda to the Bibliography I have listed only those that struck me as valuable. Mr. Burnshaw's essay qualifies my account of his relationship with Stevens (pp. 63–4). Holly Stevens' edition of the *Letters*, a work of incomparable importance to all students, contains in its introductory sections a brief but authoritative biography. Although I have taken this opportunity to correct two or three errors of fact, I have not tried to record changes of opinion or emphasis entailed by the reading and reflection of these six years.

F. K.

BIBLIOGRAPHY

Note

*In all cases in which more than one edition of any work is listed, all references in the text are to the edition marked * in this Bibliography.*

I. WALLACE STEVENS

1. Verse

Harmonium. New York 1923; New York 1931 (with additional poems).

Ideas of Order. New York, 1935 (Alcestis Press edn.); New York 1936 (A. A. Knopf trade edn.).

Owl's Clover. New York 1936.

The Man with the Blue Guitar and Other Poems. New York 1937 (with the revised version of *Owl's Clover*).

Parts of a World. New York 1942.

Notes Toward a Supreme Fiction. Cummington (Mass.) 1942.

Esthétique du Mal. Cummington (Mass.) 1944.

Transport to Summer. New York 1947. Includes *Notes Toward a Supreme Fiction* and *Esthétique du Mal.*

A Primitive like an Orb. New York 1948.

The Auroras of Autumn. New York 1950. Includes *A Primitive like an Orb.*

Selected Poems. London 1953.

Collected Poems. New York 1954. Includes a new section, *The Rock.*

Collected Poems. London 1955. (The Faber edn.; sheets of the N.Y. 1954 (Knopf) edn. bound in England.)

Opus Posthumous. Poems, Plays, Prose by Wallace Stevens. Edited, with an Introduction, by Samuel French Morse. New York 1957. Includes Stevens' three plays, some early poems, some drafts and rejected stanzas, some poems excluded from the canon by Stevens, a few left out of *C.P.* by accident, and the last poems, written after publication of *C.P.*

Opus Posthumous. London 1959. (Faber edition from sheets of Knopf edition in the previous entry.)

2. Prose

The Necessary Angel. New York 1951. Includes: "The Noble Rider and the Sound of Words," first published in *The Language of Poetry,* ed. Allen Tate, Princeton, 1942; "The Figure of the

Youth as Virile Poet," first published in *Sewanee Review*, LII
(1944); "Three Academic Pieces," consisting of a prose introduction and three poems, first published in *Partisan Review*, XV
(1947) and by the Cummington Press, Mass., (1947); "About
One of Marianne Moore's Poems," first published as "About
one of Miss Moore's Poems," *Quarterly Review of Literature*, IV
(1948); "Effects of Analogy," first published in *Yale Review*,
XXXVIII (1948); "Imagination As Value," first published in
English Institute Essays 1948, New York (1949); "The Relations
between Poetry and Painting," first published by the Museum
of Modern Art, New York 1951.

The Necessary Angel. London 1960. (Faber edn. from Knopf N.Y. 1951
edn.)

*Opus Posthumous. New York 1957. Includes *Adagia*, a few of which
had been previously published as "Materia Poetica," *View*, I
(1940); "A Collect of Philosophy," intended for a journal of
philosophy but rejected by the editor—see Morse, Preface, p.
xxxvi; "Two of Three Ideas"; "The Irrational Element in
Poetry"; and sixteen miscellaneous shorter pieces.

Opus Posthumous. London 1959.

Poems, selected, and with an Introduction, by S. F. Morse. New York
1959 (Vintage Books).

II. OTHERS

1. Books and Articles on Wallace Stevens

ALVAREZ, A.: *The Shaping Spirit*, London 1958, pp. 124–39.

BENAMON, M.: "Le Thème du Héros dans la Poésie de Wallace
Stevens," *Etudes Anglaises*, XII (1959), pp. 222–30.

BEWLEY, MARIUS: *The Complex Fate*, London 1952, pp. 171–92.

BLACKMUR, R. P.: *Form and Value in Modern Poetry*, New York 1957,
pp. 183–223.

DOGGETT, FRANK: "Wallace Stevens's Later Poetry," *E.L.H.*, XXV
(1958), pp. 137–54.

DONOGHUE, DENIS: *The Third Voice*, Princeton 1959. (Deals briefly
with Stevens' plays, pp. 193–4.)

ELLMANN, R.: "Wallace Stevens' Ice-Cream," *Kenyon Review*, XIX
(1957), pp. 89–105.

FORD, CHARLES HENRI: "Verlaine in Hartford," *View*, I (1940).

FRANKENBERG, LLOYD: *Pleasure Dome*. Cambridge (Mass.) 1949, pp.
197–267.

FRASER, G. S.: "Mind all Alone," *New Statesman*, 9 Jan. 1960, pp.
43–4.

HAYS, H. R.: "Laforgue and Wallace Stevens," *Romanic Review*, XXV
(1934), pp. 242–8.

HERINGMAN, B.: "Wallace Stevens: The Use of Poetry," *E.L.H.*, XVI (1949), pp. 325–36.

Historical Reviews of Berks County, XXIV, 4 (Fall 1959). Wallace Stevens number with biographical number.

JARRELL, R. *Poetry and the Age*, London 1955, pp. 124–36.

KREYMBORG, A.: *Our Singing Strength*, New York 1929, pp. 500–4.

MARTZ, L. L.: "The World of Wallace Stevens," *Focus*, V, London 1950, 94–109.

——"Wallace Stevens: The World as Meditation," *Yale Review*, XLVII (1958), pp. 517–36.

MIZENER, A.: "Not in Cold Blood," *Kenyon Review*, XIII (1951), pp. 218–25.

MONROE, HARRIET: *A Poet's Life*, New York 1938.

MOORE, MARIANNE: *Predilections*, London 1956, pp. 32–46.

MORSE, S. F.: "The Native Element," *Kenyon Review*, XX (1958), pp. 446–65.

——*Checklist of the Published Writings of Wallace Stevens*, Yale 1954.

O'CONNOR, W. VAN: *The Shaping Spirit*, Chicago 1950.

PACK, ROBERT: *Wallace Stevens*, New Brunswick (N.J.) 1958.

PEARCE, R. H.: "Wallace Stevens: The Life of the Imagination," *Publications of the Modern Language Association of America*, LXVI (1951), pp. 561–82.

——"Stevens Posthumous," *International Literary Annual*, II, London 1959, pp. 65–89.

QUINN, M. BERNADETTA: *The Metamorphic Tradition in Modern Poetry*, New Brunswick (N.J.) 1955, pp. 49–88.

RANSOM, JOHN CROWE: *The World's Body*, New York 1938, pp. 55–75.

SCHWARTZ, DELMORE: "Instructed of Much Mortality," *Sewanee Review*, LIV (1946) 439–49.

SIMONS, HI: "The Comedian as the Letter C," *Southern Review*, V (1940), pp. 453–68.

——"Wallace Stevens and Mallarmé," *Modern Philology*, XLIII (1946), pp. 235–59.

SOUTHWORTH, J. G.: *Some Modern American Poets*, Oxford 1950.

STALLKNECHT, N. P.: "Absence in Reality: A Study in the Epistemology of The Blue Guitar," *Kenyon Review*, XXI (1959), pp. 545–62.

SYMONS, JULIAN: "A Short View of Wallace Stevens," *Life and Letters Today*, XXVI (1946), pp. 215–24.

TAUPIN, RENÉ: *L'Influence du Symbolisme Français sur la Poésie Américaine*, Paris 1929.

WATTS, H. H.: "Wallace Stevens and the Rock of Summer," *Kenyon Review*, XIV (1952), pp. 122–40.

WILLIAMS, WILLIAM CARLOS: *Kora in Hell*, Boston 1920.

WINTERS, YVOR: *In Defense of Reason*, Denver n.d., London 1960, esp. pp. 431–59.

2. Other Works Cited

BERGSON, HENRI: *Matière et mémoire*, Paris, 1896. *Essai sur les données immédiates de la conscience*, Paris 1889.
——*Les deux Sources de la morale et de la religion* (3rd edn.), Paris 1933.
——*La Pensée et le mouvant*, Paris 1934.
FOCILLON, HENRI: *Vie des formes*, Paris 1947. (*The Life of Forms in Art*, New Haven 1942.)
HULME, T. E.: *Speculations*, London 1923.
SANTAYANA, GEORGE: *The Sense of Beauty*, London 1896.
——*Reason in Art* (*The Life of Reason*, IV), New York 1905.
——*Three Philosophical Poets*, Cambridge (Mass.) 1910.
——*Interpretations of Poetry and Religion* (2nd edn.), New York 1916.
——*The Philosophy of George Santayana*, ed. P. A. Schilpp, Evanston 1940.
——*My Host the World*, London 1953.
VALÉRY, PAUL: *Collected Works*, ed. Jackson Mathews, New York and London, 1958–   ; Vol. IV (*Dialogues*) with two Prefaces (to *Eupalinos* and *Dance and the Soul*) by Wallace Stevens. (These Prefaces are reprinted in *Opus Posthumous*.)
WAHL, JEAN: *Poésie, Pensée, Perception* (4th edn.), Paris 1948.

III. CHECKLIST

MORSE, S. F.: *Wallace Stevens: a preliminary Checklist of his pub writings, 1898–1954*. New Haven 1954.

ADDENDA

II. OTHERS

1. Books and Articles on Wallace Stevens

PEARCE, R. H.: *The Continuity of American Poetry*, Princeton 1961.
TINDALL, W. Y.: *Wallace Stevens*, Minneapolis 1961.
BURNSHAW, STANLEY: "Wallace Stevens and the Statue," *Sewanee Review*, LXIX (1961), pp. 355–66.
KERMODE, FRANK: "Notes toward a Supreme Fiction: A Commentary," *Annali dell' Istituo Universitario Orientale di Napoli* (*Sezione Germanich*), IV (1961), pp. 173–201.
BROWN, A. and HALLER, R. S.: *The Achievement of Wallace Stevens: a Critical Anthology*, Philadelphia 1962.

Boroff, Marie: *Wallace Stevens: a Collection of Critical Essays*, Englewood Cliffs (N.J.) 1963.

Pearce, R. H. and Miller, J. Hillis, *The Act of Mind, Essays on the Poetry of Wallace Stevens*, Baltimore 1965.

III. CHECKLIST

Morse, S. F., Bryer, J. R. and Riddell, J. N., *Wallace Stevens Checklist*, Denver 1963.

IV. LETTERS

Stevens, Wallace, *Selected Letters*, ed. Holly Stevens, New York and London 1966.